super-cute
macarons

super-cute
macarons

Bake and decorate delicious treats for any occasion

Loretta Liu

photography by
Maja Smend

RYLAND PETERS & SMALL
LONDON • NEW YORK

Designers Iona Hoyle and Paul Stradling
Editor Kate Eddison
Production Controller Meskerem Berhane
Art Director Leslie Harrington
Editorial Director Julia Charles
Publisher Cindy Richards

Prop Stylist Tony Hutchinson
Food Stylist Loretta Liu
Indexer Hilary Bird

First published in 2014 by Ryland Peters & Small
20–21 Jockey's Fields
London WC1R 4BW
and
519 Broadway, 5th Floor
New York NY 10012

www.rylandpeters.com

10 9 8 7 6 5 4 3 2 1

Text © Loretta Liu 2014
Design and photographs © Ryland Peters & Small 2014

ISBN: 978-1-84975-564-1

A CIP record for this book is available from
the British Library.
US Library of Congress Cataloging-in-Publication
data has been applied for.

Printed and bound in China

Notes

• Both British (Metric) and American (Imperial plus US cups) are included in these recipes for your convenience, however it is important to work with one set of measurements and not alternate between the two within a recipe.

• Macarons are very sensitive so we recommend weighing ingredients using digital scales, if possible.

• All spoon measurements are level unless otherwise specified.

• All eggs are medium (UK) or large (US) unless otherwise specified. Egg whites need to be weighed or measured precisely and aged before use.

• Uncooked or partially cooked eggs should not be served to the very old, frail, young children, pregnant women or those with compromised immune systems. You can substitute the egg whites for pasteurized egg whites (sold in cartons in supermarkets) instead.

• Ovens should be preheated to the specified temperatures. All ovens work slightly differently and macarons are very sensitive, so it is important to learn how your oven works. We recommend using an oven thermometer and suggest you consult the maker's handbook for any special instructions.

• The author uses Sugarflair food colouring pastes, so the descriptions in this book refer to this particular brand. For the exact shade, you will need to weigh or measure the colouring pastes precisely. If you use a different brand, we suggest you use the photographs in the book to match the colour. Do not use liquid food colouring in macaron shells.

contents

foreword

I first met Loretta back in 2011 not long after I opened my flagship restaurant Pollen Street Social. Loretta had started up On Café as a tribute to her good friend and I was impressed both by her determination and drive to make her business a success and quite simply by her macarons, which were a revolution in flavours and exactly what I was looking for in my restaurant at the time. We worked closely together on perfecting the perfect macarons for Pollen Street Social, dabbling in different flavours and textures and creating some unforgettable macarons.

While Loretta's macarons may look like the beautiful and vibrant traditional French macarons that we all know and love, her flavours are what make her stand apart from the rest. Loretta has drawn on her Asian inspirations and dared to dabble in spices and flavours that shock and excite. Loretta is creative and daring and this comes across in her produce; she is an inspiration to work alongside and I hope all those out there who love to bake take something from this book and step outside your comfort zone to create your own version of the perfect macaron!

Jason Atherton, May 2014

introduction

People often ask me why I choose to make macarons. They are a very tricky product to master, but there is nothing more pleasing that a batch of home-made macarons. In truth, I just love macarons. Today, we all know that we should try to avoid eating too much sugar, but I have always loved a little sweet treat. Macarons are perfect to strike this balance, as they are such tiny mouthfuls but they are rich in flavour. One little macaron will satisfy a sweet craving, and making them as gifts can bring so much joy to your friends and family. There are no secret short-cuts or cheats for achieving macaron perfection, but I believe success relies on aligning the yin and yang energies in your body – balancing gentleness and strength in your macaronage. For this book, I wanted to show the beauty that you can achieve with macarons. There is scope for so much creativity with macarons, using different colours and shapes and decorative techniques. From hand-painting to edible jewels, you can transform your macarons into works of art.

the basics

 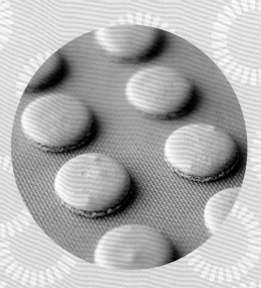

making basic French macarons

macaron making kit

To make macarons, you will need a stand mixer or mixing bowl and electric hand-held whisk, a rubber spatula, at least two flat, heavy baking sheets, a transparent silicone mat, a selection of disposable piping/pastry bags and various nozzles/tips. Please see my website (www.lorettaliu.com) for more information about equipment.

basic macarons

145 g/5 oz. egg whites

95 g/½ cup caster/superfine sugar

170 g/1⅔ cups ground almonds

260 g/2 cups minus 2 tablespoons icing/confectioners' sugar

MAKES 45

Separate the egg whites from the yolks 3–5 days before you plan to use them, and store them, covered, in the refrigerator. Do not use fresh egg whites. After 3–5 days in the refrigerator, the egg whites will be a runnier consistency (see picture opposite, top left).

Before baking, you need to bring the egg whites to room temperature.

Whisk the egg whites in a stand mixer with a whisk attachment or in a mixing bowl with a hand-held electric whisk until it has doubled in size (see picture opposite, top right). Add the caster/superfine sugar and continue to whisk until the meringue mixture looks glossy and starts to come away from the side of the bowl, forming one large blob in the middle. At this stage, if you lift the whisk, the meringue in the bowl should form a stiff peak and stay upright after the whisk has been lifted (see picture opposite, bottom left).

When you are first learning how to make macarons, it is a good idea to work with a very stiff meringue. This means that the end result can be slightly dry, but it gives you extra time when you reach the folding stage, allowing you time to get your 'macaronage' or folding technique right. If your meringue is under-whisked (or if it is perfectly whisked but you have not yet got your folding technique right), the meringue will collapse before you have incorporated all the dry ingredients.

Sift the ground almonds into a separate bowl and sift the icing/confectioners' sugar on top. Add the meringue mixture to the dry ingredients. You are now ready to fold the ingredients together (see picture opposite, bottom right).

Fold the meringue into the dry ingredients using quick circular movements until the mixture is ready for piping. This technique requires you to be gentle but not too gentle – you do not want to just coat the meringue in the dry mixture, you need to combine the two together. As well as being gentle, you also need to work quickly, otherwise the macaron mixture will lose its structure and collapse. Use a spatula to fold the ground almonds into the meringue until there are no more ground almonds around the edge of the bowl. At this stage, use your spatula to scoop up the dry ingredients from the bottom of the bowl and work them into the meringue. Fold until there are no dry ingredients visible in the bowl. The mixture should not be runny.

piping and baking macarons

using a piping bag

Transfer the mixture to a piping/pastry bag fitted with a 1-cm/½-in. round nozzle. The best way to do this without making a mess is to put the piping/pastry bag, nozzle-side down, into a jug/pitcher and scoop the mixture into it. Grip the top of the bag with the thumb and index finger of your writing hand, then, using the rest of your fingers, wrap your hand round the top of the bag. Pick the bag up and turn it over. Imagine the piping bag is an apple and you are holding the stalk between your thumb and index finger, and using the rest of your fingers to grab the apple (see picture opposite, top right).

Squeeze the mixture gently, until it is tight in the piping/pastry bag and there is no air trapped inside. Use your other hand to pull the top of the bag gently, if needed, to tighten the bag. Now you are ready to pipe. You only pipe with your writing hand; your other hand should just guide the nozzle, but not squeeze. You can only control the amount you pipe by using one hand.

Place your template on a flat, heavy baking sheet and place a transparent silicone mat on top, so that you can see the template through the mat. You can use a sheet of baking parchment instead, but this isn't advised if you are using a fan oven, as the sheets can end up blowing around the oven. Position the nozzle/tip right in the middle of the circle and pipe in the same place, until the macaron mixture pushes out to the edge of the circle (see picture opposite, bottom left). Stop piping and quickly flick the nozzle/tip up and away.

resting your macarons

At this stage, if you touch the macaron with your finger, it will be very sticky. Therefore, you need to let the macarons rest for 15–30 minutes before you cook them. After this time, a layer of skin will have formed over the top of the macarons. When the macarons go in the oven, the hot air pushes against the crust and creates the typical macaron shape with the classic 'foot' at the bottom.

baking your macarons

Meanwhile, preheat the oven to 160°C (325°F) Gas 3. Bake the macarons, one sheet at a time, on the middle shelf of the preheated oven for 8 minutes, or for the length of time it advises in the recipe. The tops of the macarons should be crisp and the undersides should be dry (see picture opposite, bottom right). It's very important to get to know your oven. I like to compare your relationship with your oven to any personal relationship. Get to know how your oven behaves and learn to work with it for a harmonious relationship. Remember that all ovens are different – you have to learn where the hot spots are and how quickly it heats up. Your oven won't change, so learn what works best and adapt the cooking time and temperature accordingly.

Allow the macarons to cool for 30 minutes on the baking sheets. This allows the sugar to crystallize and stops the macarons from getting stuck. (If the macarons have stuck to the sheet, it means that the meringue collapsed slightly and wasn't able to support the ground almonds. Try working with a stiffer meringue, until your folding technique has improved.) After 30 minutes, remove the macarons using a palette knife/metal spatula.

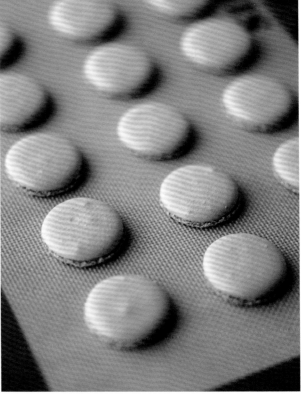

how to make a template

There are various templates provided at the back of the book on pages 138–141. To make your template, trace the template onto a piece of baking parchment the size of your baking sheet and repeat for as many as you can fit, leaving a gap between them. You can fit about 12 standard 5-cm/2-in. rounds on an average baking sheet. Please see my website (www.lorettaliu.com) for more information about templates.

piping hearts

Heart-shaped macarons make a charming Valentine's gift. See recipe, page 73.

To pipe hearts, you will need to use a slightly smaller nozzle/tip than you would use if you were piping rounds. I find 8-mm/⅜-in. is a good size for this task.

Trace the Heart template from page 139 onto some baking parchment to create about 12 hearts, or as many as you can fit on your baking sheet. Place the template onto a flat, heavy baking sheet and place a transparent silicone mat on top so that you can see the Heart template through it.

Position the nozzle at the top left of the heart, pipe down to the bottom then up to the top left of the heart, and move the nozzle back down again to make sure that the template is filled. Stop piping and quickly flick the nozzle/tip up and away from the macaron surface (see pictures, opposite).

piping face shapes

For most animal shapes, I use a standard 5-cm/2-in. round template. Trace the template from page 138 onto some baking parchment to create about 12 circles, or as many as you can fit on your baking sheet. Place the template onto a flat, heavy baking sheet and place a transparent silicone mat on top so that you can see the template through it.

Pointy ears

For pointy ears such as cats' ears (see recipe, page 45), follow the instructions on page 12 for piping rounds. Once you have piped a round, use a sugar-working tool or cocktail stick/toothpick to drag the macaron mixture away from the circle into a pointy ear (see pictures, opposite). Repeat for the second ear.

Round ears

For round ears, such as bears' ears (see recipe, page 42), follow the instructions on page 12 for piping rounds. Once you have piped a round, use a smaller nozzle/tip to pipe a blob of macaron mixture for each ear that is just touching the edge of the main circle.

Long ears

For long ears, such as bunnies' ears (see recipe, page 54), follow the instructions on page 12 for piping rounds. Once you have piped a round, use a small nozzle and start piping at the top of the ear, working towards the piped macaron circle. When you reach the piped circle, stop piping and quickly flick the nozzle/tip up and away from the macaron surface.

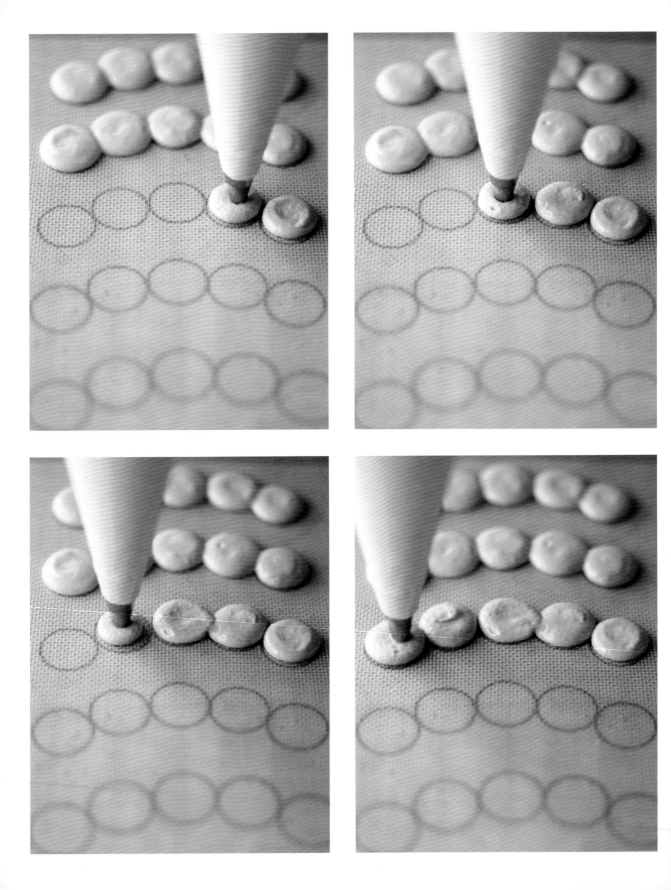

piping joined macarons

For joined macarons, such as smacs (see recipe, page 126) or caterpillars (see recipe, page 49), trace the template from page 138 (Caterpillar) or page 141 (Smac) onto some baking parchment to create as many as you can fit on your baking sheet.

Place the template onto a flat, heavy baking sheet and place a transparent silicone mat on top so that you can see the template through it.

Pipe each macaron individually, following the instructions on page 12. Position the nozzle/tip right in the middle of the circle and pipe in the same place, until the macaron mixture pushes out to the edge of the circle. Stop piping and quickly flick the nozzle/tip up and away from the macaron surface (see pictures, opposite).

The macarons should not join together while you are piping them – this will occur when the macaron mixture expands during resting.

Macaron pops
Try placing a lollipop stick in the filling of your joined macarons to create a fun macaron pop!

filling macarons

Filling macarons is the fun bit. There is such a vast range of fillings you can use, and you certainly don't have to stick to the ones suggested in this book. It is best to make a basic, unflavoured macaron shell and add all the flavour into the filling. This is because the macaron mixture is so delicate and so unforgiving that the smallest addition of liquid or oil or another dry ingredient can ruin the batter and affect your macaron shells. If you do want to add a flavour to your shells, I suggest a tiny amount of strongly flavoured essence oils, which will not affect the batter too much.

Simple filling ideas
Try these quick and easy options for instant fillings:
• jam/jelly or fruit preserves
• chocolate and hazelnut spread
• fruit curds, such as lemon curd
• nut butters, such as peanut butter

How to fill macarons
Firstly, match up your macaron shells into pairs of the same shape and size. Line them up in rows of pairs, placing one shell from each pair flat-side up and the other flat-side down.

For perfect circles of filling, you can use a piping/pastry bag fitted with a small round nozzle/tip. This enables you to make professional-looking morsels, but can be fiddly and you will waste some of your filling in the piping/pastry bag. I suggest using a palette knife or metal spatula to spread the filling onto the shells. You will need about a teaspoonful of filling for standard macaron shells.

Pipe or spread the filling onto the flat-side of one macaron shell in each pair, then top with the flat-side of the other shell, pressing them together gently. Allow to set in the refrigerator for 12 hours, unless the filling contains fresh fruit, in which case the filled macarons should be chilled for only 1–2 hours.

white chocolate ganache

230 g/1½ cups good-quality white chocolate, broken into pieces (use Valrhona Opalys or Ivoire, for the best results)

120 ml/8 tablespoons whipping cream

50 g/3½ tablespoons unsalted butter

MAKES 500 G/18 OZ.

Melt the chocolate in a microwave or in a heatproof bowl set over a pan of barely simmering water, stirring regularly.

Place the cream in a saucepan and heat over medium heat until it is just about to boil. Pour about one-third of the cream over the chocolate and stir with a rubber spatula gently, until blended. Add a little more cream, and stir again until smooth. Keep adding the cream gradually, until you have added it all and the mixture is silky and smooth.

Allow the ganache to cool to 30°C/86°F, the stir in the butter, a little at a time. If you add the butter when the ganache is too hot, it will split.

Cover the ganache with clingfilm/plastic wrap, pressing it onto the surface of the ganache to stop a skin from forming. Allow to cool to room temperature, then leave in a cold place for 24 hours. Ganache doesn't react well to being stored in the refrigerator, so I suggest a cold room of your house. However, in the summer, or if your house is warm, you will need to use the refrigerator.

After this time, the ganache should be a spreadable consistency.

Choosing white chocolate for ganache
White Chocolate Ganache is very difficult to get right when following a recipe, as the consistency of white chocolate varies so much from manufacturer to manufacturer. This recipe is specifically for using the varieties mentioned in the ingredients list, Valrhona Opalys or Ivoire. You can buy it online. If you use a different brand of white chocolate, the results will vary.

chocolate ganache

200 g/1⅓ cups good-quality dark/bittersweet chocolate, broken into pieces (use chocolate with 70% cocoa solids, such as Valrhona Guanaja, for the best results)

120 ml/8 tablespoons whipping cream

50 g/3½ tablespoons unsalted butter

MAKES 500 G/18 OZ.

Melt the chocolate in a microwave or in a heatproof bowl set over a pan of barely simmering water, stirring regularly.

Place the cream in a saucepan and heat over medium heat until it is just about to boil. Pour about one-third of the cream over the chocolate and stir with a rubber spatula gently, until blended. Add a little more cream, and stir again until smooth. Keep adding the cream gradually, until you have added it all and the mixture is silky and smooth.

Allow the ganache to cool to 30°C/86°F, the stir in the butter, a little at a time. If you add the butter when the ganache is too hot, it will split.

Cover the ganache with clingfilm/plastic wrap, pressing it onto the surface of the ganache to stop a skin from forming. Allow to cool to room temperature, then leave in a cold place for 24 hours. Ganache doesn't react well to being stored in the refrigerator, so I suggest a cold room of your house. However, in the summer, or if your house is warm, you will need to use the refrigerator.

After this time, the ganache should be a spreadable consistency.

Choosing the right cream
Whipping cream has a fat content somewhere between single/light and double/heavy cream, which makes it ideal for making ganache. Double/heavy cream is very oily and can split, and single/light cream doesn't contain enough fat.

custard cream

4 egg yolks

80 g/6½ tablespoons caster/
superfine sugar

20 g/2⅓ tablespoons plain/
all-purpose flour, sifted

20 g/3 tablespoons cornflour/
cornstarch, sifted

425 ml/generous 1¾ cups full-fat/
whole milk

½ teaspoon vanilla bean paste

icing/confectioners' sugar, to dust

MAKES 500 G/18 OZ.

Whisk together the egg yolks and sugar in a heatproof bowl, until they turn a pale yellow. Whisk in the flour and cornflour/cornstarch.

Place the milk and vanilla bean paste in a saucepan and bring to a gentle simmer over low heat, stirring frequently. As soon as it reaches a simmer, remove the pan from the heat and let cool for 30 seconds.

Slowly pour half of the hot milk onto the egg mixture, whisking all the time to prevent the eggs from scrambling. Return the mixture to the remaining milk in the pan, whisking constantly.

Bring the mixture back to the boil and simmer for 1 minute, or until smooth, whisking constantly.

Pour the cream into a clean bowl and dust with icing sugar to prevent a skin forming. Allow to cool to room temperature, then refrigerate until needed.

caramel chocolate ganache

150 g/scant 1 cup good-quality
blond chocolate, broken into
pieces (use Valrhona dulcey for
the best results)

300 ml/1¼ cups whipping cream

180 g/1 cup minus 1½ tablespoons
caster/granulated sugar

1 teaspoon vanilla powder

50 g/3½ tablespoons unsalted
butter

1½ teaspoons salt

MAKES 650 G/23 OZ.

Place the cream in a saucepan and heat over medium heat until just about to boil.

Place the sugar in a saucepan and heat, without stirring, until the sugar has melted and you have a golden caramel. Swirl the pan occasionally, if needed. Add the hot cream and stir to mix. Use a sugar thermometer to measure the temperature, then heat over medium heat until the mixture reaches 104°C/219°F. As soon as it reaches this temperature, remove the caramel from the heat and immerse the bottom of the pan briefly in a sink of cold water to stop the cooking.

Let the temperature drop to 75°C/167°F, then add, a little at a time, to the chocolate. Stir well after each addition to make sure the chocolate is fully melted.

When the mixture reaches 35°C/95°F, add the softened butter and blend. Allow to cool to room temperature, then leave in a cold place for 24 hours. Ganache doesn't react well to being stored in the refrigerator, so I suggest a cold room of your house. However, in the summer, you may need to use the refrigerator.

buttercream

300 g/1½ cups caster/superfine
sugar

5 large/US extra large egg whites

500 g/4½ sticks unsalted butter,
cut into pieces

2 teaspoons vanilla powder or
seeds of 1 vanilla pod/bean

MAKES 800 G/28 OZ.

Place the sugar and egg whites into the bowl of a stand mixer or a heatproof mixing bowl and set over a pan of gently simmering water. Whisk using a hand-held electric whisk for 3 minutes, until the sugar has dissolved and the egg whites are hot to the touch. Transfer the bowl to the stand mixer fitted with the whisk attachment, if using. Whisk on high speed in the mixer or with a hand-held electric whisk, until the mixture has cooled down and formed stiff peaks; about 8 minutes.

Switch to the paddle attachment. Add the butter, one piece at a time, and beat until incorporated. Don't worry if the mixture appears curdled after all the butter has been added; it will become smooth again with beating. Beat until smooth.

If using within several hours, cover with clingfilm/plastic wrap and keep in a cool room. Alternatively, store in the refrigerator for 3 days. Beat to soften before use.

decorating techniques

There are so many ways to transform a simple macaron into a work of edible art. From painting and icing to sugar decorations and stacking, this book is full of impressive ideas.

hand-painting

You can create stunning effects on a macaron with a clean paintbrush. To create edible paint, you just need to dilute a small amount of food colouring paste (about ½ teaspoon) in a few drops of food colouring paste rejuvenator spirit/thinner.
This can be bought online or in specialist cake decorating stores. Add enough to create a liquid paint, mixing well.

Use a clean flat paintbrush for large brush strokes and a fine paintbrush for thin lines. You can paint flowers or abstract designs or whatever you choose.

Try different shapes and sizes of brush for different effects; just remember to make sure it is clean and hasn't been used for non-edible paints!

royal icing

90 g/3⅛ oz. egg whites

480 g/3⅓ cups icing/confectioners' sugar

2 tablespoons freshly squeezed lemon juice

MAKES ABOUT 570 G/20 OZ.

Place all of the ingredients into the bowl of a stand mixer fitted with the paddle attachment, and beat for 5–7 minutes, until white and thick. Alternatively, use a mixing bowl and hand-held electric whisk.

If you are not using it immediately, cover the icing with clingfilm/plastic wrap, pressing it onto the surface to prevent a skin from forming and to stop it from drying out. Store in the refrigerator until needed.

working with royal icing

Royal icing can be used to decorate macarons with line art, it can be used to create run-outs, and it is also very useful as the edible 'glue' for sticking embellishments onto macaron shells or for assembling shells in stacks. It's quite difficult to make a small batch of icing, as a small amount of egg white is tricky to whisk. Therefore, it is better to make the batch above even if it means you may waste some. It's better than trying to make a small batch and wasting it all!

Colouring royal icing
Add food colouring paste using a cocktail stick/toothpick and stir until the icing is an even shade. Add the food colouring a little at a time, as you can always add more! If you need multiple colours, split the batch of icing into portions in separate bowls and colour each one individually.

Piping royal icing
Use a small disposable piping/pastry bag and snip of the end to create a small hole. It is a good idea to practise piping onto a sheet of baking parchment before you start piping onto your macaron shells.

Making a paper piping/pastry bag
You can make a simple piping/pastry bag for icing from a sheet of baking parchment. Simply roll the parchment into a cone.

adding embellishments

There is a huge variety of sugar decorations available today, which are sold in supermarkets and specialist baking stores, as well as from online retailers. A pair of tweezers is useful for placing decorations onto macaron shells, so it's a good idea to buy a pair that you keep just for baking purposes. In the Precious Gifts chapter, different sugar decorations are used to create pretty effects. With a steady hand, it is easier than it looks to achieve shimmering, edible decorations.

Adding sugar diamonds and pearls
To stick sugar jewels onto macarons, such as the Turquoise with Pearls (page 91), you will need to prepare a batch of Royal Icing (see page 29). Put the icing in a small disposable piping/pastry bag and snip off the end to create a small hole. Pipe a dot of Royal Icing onto the centre of the macaron shell. Use it to stick a sugar diamond to the shell. Stick sugar pearls around the diamonds using more dots of Royal Icing. Use tweezers if necessary for very small decorations. Allow to dry for 1 hour.

using sugarpaste

Sugarpaste/fondant is also known as ready-to-roll icing. It can be bought in various colours, but for this book it is best to buy white sugarpaste/fondant and add your own colouring. This is firstly because it gives you much more control over the colour you use, and you can make your colour darker, more vibrant or paler to suit your needs. It is also because you will often need only a very small amount of sugarpaste/fondant, so you can just cut off the amount you need and seal the rest up tightly for another time.

Colouring sugarpaste/fondant
If you want to colour your sugarpaste/fondant, use a cocktail stick/toothpick to add a small amount of food colouring paste (or use the amount specified in the recipe, if it specifies an exact amount). Place the sugarpaste/fondant on a clean work surface dusted with icing/confectioners' sugar, and knead it until it is an even shade. Remember, use a little bit of food colouring paste first – you can always add more food colouring paste if needed, but you cannot take it away!

Creating shapes
Dust the surface well with icing/confectioners' sugar and use a rolling pin to roll the sugarpaste out to the desired thickness. Use mini cutters to cut out shapes such as hearts or flowers, and set them aside to dry before use.

using a lace technique

This is a simple technique that creates very impressive results. Packs of cake lace can be bought from online retailers, and they come with specific instructions on how to use the particular brand (see Suppliers, page 143). However, the basic technique is as follows:

Place the recommended amount of water in the bowl of a stand mixer fitted with a whisk attachment (or use a mixing bowl and hand-held electric whisk) and add the amount of powder specified on the packet instructions.

Mix on medium-high speed for 2 minutes, or as recommended, then add the amount of liquid specified on the packet instructions.

Mix on medium-high speed for 5–8 minutes, or until the mixture is smooth.

Pour the mixture onto the lace silicone mat and spread it out using a knife. Make sure there is cake lace mixture in all the moulds, then use the knife to remove the excess mixture.

Allow to dry at room temperature for 6–8 hours or place in a very low oven for 10–15 minutes.

To release the lace, place the mould face-down on a sheet of baking parchment and peel the mould away, using a knife to help you release the cake lace.

To adhere the lace to your macaron shells, moisten the macaron shell with a little water, then press the lace on to it and allow to dry.

assembling macarons

There is much more to macarons than a pair of macaron shells, sandwiched together around a filling. You can stack shells to create animal bodies, as shown in the Sleepy Cats (page 45), Little Pigs (page 46) and Pandas (page 57). You can also create multi-layer faces to give depth and character to your animals, such as the Teddy Bears (page 42), where the nose is made from a smaller macaron shell.

Decorate the face first, then allow the Royal Icing to dry so that you don't smudge it when you stick it to the body. Make the body with 2 shells of the same colour and sandwich them together with a filling.

Use Royal Icing to stick the head onto the body, then allow to dry before serving.

You can also stick the head onto the side on the body (see Sleepy Cats, page 45), or make the heads with a smaller template (see Little Pigs, page 46). Experiment with different animals and you will come up with your own ideas for assembling macarons.

pinning macarons

On page 82, there is a gorgeous recipe for a Macaron Flower Pot. It will wow guests at a spring party or make a pleasing gift for Mother's Day. Here is how to achieve this impressive technique.

You will need a polystyrene ball for the centre of the flowers, a plastic stalk, a small plant pot and some dry rice.

Insert the plastic stick into the polystyrene ball. Fill the plant pot with rice, then place the stick into the pot, making sure that there is enough rice around it to allow it to stand securely. You do not want to see your beautiful creation topple over when people are grabbing macarons!

Use a clean paintbrush to paint the polystyrene ball with Chocolate Ganache (see page 23) or Royal Icing (see page 29), making sure the ball is evenly covered all over.

Assemble your macarons with their filling and allow them to set for 1 hour. Insert a cocktail stick/toothpick into each macaron, making sure that it does not go all the way through the macaron.

storing macarons

The batches of macaron mixture may seem quite large for making at home. This is because macaron batter is very unstable and unforgiving, and it is very difficult to make it successfully in small batches. Therefore, I recommend you always make a full batch.

You must always make a complete batch for each colour, as the colouring is folded in during the macaronage and the macaronage works best when done on a full batch. Therefore you may have lots of macarons left over. Luckily, macarons last for 3–5 days in the refrigerator and they also freeze very well. Once filled with Ganache or Buttercream, you can freeze the macarons, but do not freeze any macarons containing fresh cream or fresh fruit.

animal magic

These adorable teddy faces will delight adults and children alike. The design is simple but effective, making these a great option for your first attempt at super-cute macarons.

teddy bears

FOR THE MACARON SHELLS
2 batches Basic Macarons
(see recipe, page 11)

4 g/¾ teaspoon dark brown food colouring paste

1.5 g/¼ teaspoon chestnut food colouring paste

0.5 g/scant ⅛ teaspoon red food colouring paste

TO DECORATE
1 batch Royal Icing (see recipe, page 29)

2.5 g/½ teaspoon dark brown food colouring paste

120 pearl sugar balls

disposable piping/pastry bag fitted with a 1-cm/½-in. round nozzle/tip

2 disposable piping/pastry bags fitted with 6-mm/¼-in. round nozzles/tips

5-cm/2-in. round template (see page 138)

transparent silicone mat

2.5-cm/1-in. round template (see page 138)

small disposable piping/pastry bag for icing

MAKES 60

Preheat the oven to 160°C (325°F) Gas 3.

Prepare the first batch of Basic Macarons according to the recipe on page 11, but add the dark brown food colouring paste before folding the egg whites into the dry ingredients. Put three-quarters of the mixture into a piping/pastry bag fitted with a 1-cm/½-in. round nozzle/tip, and put the remaining one-quarter of the mixture into another piping/pastry bag fitted with a 6-mm/¼-in. round nozzle/tip.

Place the 5-cm/2-in. round template on a baking sheet, and place a transparent silicone mat on top. Using the piping/pastry bag fitted with the 1-cm/½-in. nozzle, pipe the round face of the bear onto the silicone mat, using the template as a guide. Pipe the ears of the bear using the piping/pastry bag with the 6-mm/¼-in. nozzle. Repeat to make 60 bears (you will need more than one baking sheet).

Tap the bottom of the sheets lightly on the work surface to settle the mixture. Carefully slide the template out from under the silicone mat. Leave the macarons to rest for 15–30 minutes.

Bake the macarons, one sheet at a time, on the middle shelf of the preheated oven for 8 minutes, until the tops are crisp and the undersides of the macarons are dry. Leave to cool for 30 minutes on the baking sheets. Leave the oven on.

Meanwhile, prepare the second batch of Basic Macarons according to the recipe on page 11, but add the chestnut and red food colouring pastes before folding the egg whites into the dry ingredients. Put the mixture into a piping/pastry bag fitted with a 6-mm/¼-in. nozzle/tip.

Place the 2.5-cm/1-in. template on a baking sheet, and put the silicone mat on top. Pipe the round noses for the bears, using the template as a guide. Repeat to make 60 noses (you may need more than one baking sheet). Tap the bottom of the sheets lightly on the work surface to settle the mixture. Carefully slide the template out from under the silicone mat. Leave the macarons to rest for 15–30 minutes.

Bake the macarons, one sheet at a time, on the middle shelf of the preheated oven for 6 minutes, until the tops are crisp and the undersides of the macarons are dry. Leave to cool for 30 minutes on the baking sheets.

To decorate
Make the Royal Icing recipe, adding the dark brown food colouring paste. Transfer to a small piping/pastry bag for icing, and snip off the end to create a small hole.

Stick the noses onto the bears' faces, using a little Royal Icing to fix the noses in place. Pipe eyes and a mouth onto each teddy bear with Royal Icing. Stick a pearl sugar decoration onto each ear, using a small amount of Royal Icing to fix it in place. Leave to dry for 1 hour.

Decide for yourself what expression to give your kitties. You can opt for whatever colour you like by experimenting with different food colouring pastes.

sleepy cats

FOR THE MACARON SHELLS
3 batches Basic Macarons (see recipe, page 11)

3 g/⅔ teaspoon tangerine food colouring paste

4 g/¾ teaspoon dark brown food colouring paste

4 g/¾ teaspoon spruce green food colouring paste

FOR THE FILLING
1 batch Chocolate Ganache (see recipe, page 23)

1 tablespoon peppermint essence oil

TO DECORATE
20 g/¾ oz. white sugarpaste/fondant

baby pink and/or orange food colouring paste

1 batch Royal Icing (see recipe, page 29)

black food colouring paste

4 disposable piping/pastry bags fitted with 1-cm/½-in. round nozzles/tips

5-cm/2-in. round template (see page 138)

transparent silicone mat

tiny heart and flower cutters

small disposable piping/pastry bag for icing

MAKES 30

Preheat the oven to 160°C (325°F) Gas 3.

Prepare the first batch of Basic Macarons according to the recipe on page 11, but add the tangerine food colouring paste before folding the egg whites into the dry ingredients. Put the mixture into a piping/pastry bag fitted with a 1-cm/½-in. round nozzle/tip.

Place the 5-cm/2-in. round template on a baking sheet, and place a transparent silicone mat on top. Pipe 30 rounds onto the silicone mat, using the template as a guide. Using a cocktail stick/toothpick, drag and pull the ears from the round faces. (You will need more than one baking sheet.) Tap the bottom of the sheets lightly on the work surface to settle the mixture. Carefully slide the template out from under the silicone mat. Leave the macarons to rest for 15–30 minutes.

Bake the macarons, one sheet at a time, on the middle shelf of the preheated oven for 8 minutes, until the tops are crisp and the undersides are dry. Leave to cool for 30 minutes on the baking sheets. Leave the oven on.

Meanwhile, prepare the second batch of Basic Macarons according to the recipe on page 11, but add the dark brown food colouring paste. Place the 5-cm/2-in. round template on a baking sheet, and place a transparent silicone mat on top. Using the piping/pastry bag fitted with the 1-cm/½-in. nozzle/tip, pipe 45 rounds onto the silicone mat. (You will need more than one baking sheet.)

Tap the bottom of the sheets lightly on the work surface to settle the mixture. Carefully slide the template out from under the silicone mat. Leave the macarons to rest for 15–30 minutes. Bake the macarons, one sheet at a time, on the middle shelf of the preheated oven for 8 minutes, until the tops are crisp and the undersides are dry. Leave to cool for 30 minutes on the baking sheets. Leave the oven on.

Meanwhile, prepare the third batch of Basic Macarons according to the recipe on page 11, but add the spruce green food colouring paste. Pipe and bake 45 green macaron shells, repeating the process above.

Divide the Ganache in half. Mix the peppermint essence oil into one batch. Put the Ganache into two separate piping/pastry bags with 1-cm/½-in. nozzle/tips. Line the brown macarons into rows of 3. Pipe some plain Ganache onto the first two shells, and stack them into towers with the third, empty, shell on top. Repeat to make 15 brown stacks. Use the mint Ganache to fill the green shells and make 15 green stacks. Leave to set in the refrigerator for at least 12 hours before serving.

To decorate
Use a cocktail stick/toothpick to add a little baby pink or orange food colouring paste to the white sugarpaste/fondant. Knead until the colour is even, then roll out to a thickness of 3 mm/⅛ in. Cut out tiny hearts and flowers and leave to dry. Make the Royal Icing recipe and use a cocktail stick/toothpick to add enough black food colouring paste to create a dark shade. Transfer to a small piping/pastry bag for icing, and snip off the end to create a small hole. Pipe on whiskers, eyes and noses. Allow to dry for 20 minutes. Use the rest of the icing to stick on the hearts and flowers, then to stick the faces to the bodies. Leave to dry for 1 hour.

Using two different sizes of macaron gives you the effect of having a head and body of an animal, as shown here with these pigs. I also use two different shades of pink to enhance the difference.

little pigs

FOR THE MACARON SHELLS
2 batches Basic Macarons (see recipe, page 11)

2.5 g/½ teaspoon dusky pink food colouring paste

3 g/⅔ teaspoon pink food colouring paste

FOR THE FILLING
1 batch Buttercream (see recipe, page 24)

3 tablespoons strawberry jam/jelly, sieved/strained

TO DECORATE
baby pink food colouring paste

30 g/1 oz white sugarpaste/fondant

1 batch Royal Icing (see recipe, page 29)

black food colouring paste

2 disposable piping/pastry bags fitted with 1-cm/½-in. round nozzles/tips

5.5-cm/2¼-in. round template (see page 138)

transparent silicone mat

4-cm/1½-in. round template (see page 138)

small disposable piping/pastry bag for icing

MAKES 40

Preheat the oven to 160°C (325°F) Gas 3.

Prepare the first batch of Basic Macarons according to the recipe on page 11, but add the dusky pink food colouring paste before folding the egg whites into the dry ingredients. Put the mixture into a piping/pastry bag fitted with a 1-cm/½-in. round nozzle/tip.

Place the 5.5-cm/2¼-in. round template on a baking sheet, and place a transparent silicone mat on top. Pipe 80 rounds onto the silicone mat, using the template as a guide. (You will need more than one baking sheet.) Tap the bottom of the sheets lightly on the work surface to settle the mixture. Carefully slide the template out from under the silicone mat. Leave the macarons to rest for 15–30 minutes.

Bake the macarons, one sheet at a time, on the middle shelf of the preheated oven for 8 minutes, until the tops are crisp and the undersides of the macarons are dry. Leave to cool for 30 minutes on the baking sheets. Leave the oven on.

Meanwhile, prepare the second batch of Basic Macarons according to the recipe on page 11, but add the pink food colouring paste before folding the egg whites into the dry ingredients. Put the mixture a piping/pastry bag fitted with a 1-cm/½-in. round nozzle/tip.

Place the 4-cm/1½-in. round template on a baking sheet, and place a transparent silicone mat on top. Pipe 40 circles, using the template as a guide. (You will need more than one baking sheet.) Tap the bottom of the sheets lightly on the work surface to settle the mixture. Carefully slide the template out from under the silicone mat. Leave the macarons to rest for 15–30 minutes.

Bake the macarons, one sheet at a time, on the middle shelf of the preheated oven for 6 minutes, until the tops are crisp and the undersides of the macarons are dry. Leave to cool for 30 minutes on the baking sheet.

To make the filling, mix the jam/jelly into the Buttercream. Line the dusky pink macarons into rows of 2, flat-side up. Using a teaspoon, place a little filling mixture onto half of the dusky pink shells, and sandwich the pairs together gently to create 40 macarons. Leave to set in the refrigerator for at least 12 hours before serving.

To decorate
Use a cocktail stick/toothpick to add some baby pink food colouring paste to the white sugarpaste/fondant. Knead until the colour is even. Shape the sugarpaste/fondant into the pigs' noses, ears and tails. Leave to dry before use.

Make the Royal Icing recipe and use a cocktail stick/toothpick to add enough black food colouring paste to create a dark shade. Transfer to a small piping/pastry bag for icing, and snip off the end to create a small hole. Pipe eyes and mouths onto the pink faces. Allow to dry for 20 minutes. Use the rest of the icing to stick the faces onto the bodies, then to attach the ears, noses and tails. Leave to dry for 1 hour.

Creating joined macarons is easier than it looks, and it allows you to make shapes like this cheerful caterpillar. The template can be found at the back of the book, but you can try making longer caterpillars, if you are feeling brave!

caterpillar

FOR THE MACARON SHELLS
2 batches Basic Macarons (see recipe, page 11)

3.5 g/generous ⅔ teaspoon gooseberry food colouring paste

3 g/⅔ teaspoon tangerine food colouring paste

FOR THE FILLING
3 tablespoons passionfruit jam/jelly

1 batch Chocolate Ganache (see recipe, page 23)

TO DECORATE
1 batch Royal Icing (see recipe, page 29)

black food colouring paste

disposable piping/pastry bag fitted with a 1-cm/½-in. round nozzle/tip

Caterpillar template (see page 138)

transparent silicone mat

Caterpillar Legs template (see page 138)

disposable piping/pastry bag fitted with a 4-mm/⅛-in. round nozzle/tip

2 small disposable piping/pastry bags for icing

MAKES 20

Preheat the oven to 160°C (325°F) Gas 3.

Prepare the first batch of Basic Macarons according to the recipe on page 11, but add the gooseberry food colouring paste before folding the egg whites into the dry ingredients. Put the mixture into a piping/pastry bag fitted with a 1-cm/½-in. round nozzle/tip.

Place the Caterpillar template on a baking sheet, and place a transparent silicone mat on top. Pipe 40 caterpillars, using the template as a guide. (You will need more than one baking sheet.) Tap the bottom of the sheets lightly on the work surface to settle the mixture. Carefully slide the template out from under the silicone mat. Leave the macarons to rest for 15–30 minutes.

Bake the macarons, one sheet at a time, on the middle shelf of the preheated oven for 8 minutes, until the tops are crisp and the undersides of the macarons are dry. Leave to cool for 30 minutes on the baking sheet. Leave the oven on.

Meanwhile, prepare the second batch of Basic Macarons according to the recipe on page 11, but add the tangerine food colouring paste before folding the egg whites into the dry ingredients. Put the mixture into a piping/pastry bag fitted with a 4-mm/⅛-in. round nozzle/tip.

Place the Caterpillar Legs template onto a baking sheet, and place a transparent silicone mat on top. Pipe 80 legs, using the template as a guide. Tap the bottom of the sheet lightly on the work surface to settle the mixture. Carefully slide the template out from under the silicone mat. Leave the macarons to rest for 15–30 minutes.

Bake the macarons, one sheet at a time, on the middle shelf of the preheated oven for 4 minutes, until the tops are crisp and the undersides of the macarons are dry. Leave to cool for 30 minutes on the baking sheet.

To make the filling, mix the jam/jelly into the ganache.

Spread filling onto the flat-side of one caterpillar shell and sandwich together with another. Repeat with the remaining macaron shells. Leave to set in the refrigerator for at least 12 hours before serving.

To decorate
Make the Royal Icing and divide it into two portions. Use a cocktail stick/toothpick to add enough black food colouring paste to one portion to create a dark shade. Transfer to a small piping/pastry bag for icing and snip off the end to create a small hole. Repeat with the white portion in another small piping/pastry bag for icing.

With the black icing, pipe eyes and mouths onto each caterpillar. Use the white icing to stick 4 legs onto each caterpillar, and then to pipe a white spot onto each eye. Finally, use the black icing again to pipe a final tiny dot onto each eye. Leave to dry for 1 hour.

These butterflies are dazzling in black and bright green, though you could opt for other colours, if you prefer. You will need a clean, flat paintbrush to paint the wings.

butterflies

FOR THE MACARON SHELLS
2 batches Basic Macarons
(see recipe, page 11)

5 g/1 teaspoon black food
colouring paste

3 g/²⁄₃ teaspoon gooseberry food
colouring paste

FOR THE FILLING
3 tablespoons salted caramel
sauce

1 batch Buttercream (see recipe,
page 24)

TO DECORATE
white colouring powder

rejuvenating spirit to dilute the
colouring powder

1 batch Royal Icing (see recipe,
page 29)

gooseberry food colouring paste

*2 disposable piping/pastry bags
fitted with 1-cm/½-in. round
nozzles/tips*

*5-cm/2-in. round template
(see page 138)*

small flat paintbrush

*small disposable piping/pastry bag
for icing*

MAKES 60

Preheat the oven to 160°C (325°F) Gas 3.

Prepare the first batch of Basic Macarons according to the recipe on page 11, but add the black food colouring paste before folding the egg whites into the dry ingredients. Put the mixture into a piping/pastry bag fitted with a 1-cm/½-in. round nozzle/tip.

Place the 5-cm/2-in. round template on a baking sheet, and place a transparent silicone mat on top. Pipe 60 rounds, using the template as a guide. (You will need more than one baking sheet.) Tap the bottom of the sheets lightly on the work surface to settle the mixture. Carefully slide the template out from under the silicone mat. Leave the macarons to rest for 15–30 minutes.

Bake the macarons, one sheet at a time, on the middle shelf of the preheated oven for 8 minutes, until the tops are crisp and the undersides of the macarons are dry. Leave to cool for 30 minutes on the baking sheet. Leave the oven on.

Meanwhile, prepare the second batch of Basic Macarons according to the recipe on page 11, but add the gooseberry food colouring paste before folding the egg whites into the dry ingredients. Put the mixture into a piping/pastry bag fitted with a 1-cm/½-in. round nozzle/tip.

Place the 5-cm/2-in. round template on a baking sheet, and place a transparent silicone mat on top. Pipe 60 rounds, using the template as a guide. (You will need more than one baking sheet.) Tap the bottom of the sheets lightly on the work surface to settle the mixture. Carefully slide the template out from under the silicone mat. Leave the macarons to rest for 15–30 minutes.

Bake the macarons, one sheet at a time, on the middle shelf of the preheated oven for 8 minutes, until the tops are crisp and the undersides of the macarons are dry. Leave to cool for 30 minutes on the baking sheet. Leave the oven on.

To make the filling, mix the caramel into the Buttercream.

Place a teaspoonful of the filling onto the flat-side of each gooseberry macaron, and top with a black macaron, pressing them together gently. Leave to set in the refrigerator for at least 12 hours before serving.

To decorate

Add a little rejuvenating spirit to the white food colouring powder to create a white food paint. Use a clean flat paintbrush to paint butterfly wings onto the black side of each macaron.

Prepare the Royal Icing and add a little gooseberry food colouring paste using a cocktail stick/toothpick. Mix until you have a vibrant green shade. Transfer to a small piping/pastry bag for icing and snip off the end to create a small hole. Pipe the bodies and antennae onto each butterfly. Leave to dry for 1 hour.

I use a zingy orange Buttercream in these vibrant yellow macarons, but you could add runny honey to the Buttercream instead, if you want to make them honey bees! Whatever the filling, these cheerful bees are a delight to make.

buzzy bees

FOR THE MACARON SHELLS
1 quantity Basic Macarons (see recipe, page 11)

3 g/⅔ teaspoon egg yellow food colouring paste

FOR THE FILLING
1 batch Buttercream (see recipe, page 24)

3 tablespoons orange marmalade

TO DECORATE
1 quantity Royal Icing (see recipe, page 29)

black food colouring paste

disposable piping/pastry bag fitted with a 1-cm/½-in. round nozzle/tip

6-cm/2⅜-in. round template (see page 138)

small disposable piping/pastry bag for icing

MAKES 30

Preheat the oven to 160°C (325°F) Gas 3.

Prepare the Basic Macarons according to the recipe on page 11, but add the egg yellow food colouring paste before folding the egg whites into the dry ingredients. Put the mixture into a piping/pastry bag fitted with a 1-cm/½-in. round nozzle/tip.

Place the 6-cm/2⅜-in. round template on a baking sheet, and place a transparent silicone mat on top. Pipe 60 rounds, using the template as a guide. (You will need more than one baking sheet.) Tap the bottom of the sheets lightly on the work surface to settle the mixture. Carefully slide the template out from under the silicone mat. Leave the macarons to rest for 15–30 minutes.

Bake the macarons, one sheet at a time, on the middle shelf of the preheated oven for 8 minutes, until the tops are crisp and the undersides of the macarons are dry. Leave to cool for 30 minutes on the baking sheet.

For the filling, mix the orange marmalade into the Buttercream.

Spread a teaspoonful of the filling mixture onto the flat-sides of half of the shells, and top with the remaining macaron shells, pressing together gently. Leave to set in the refrigerator for at least 12 hours before serving.

To decorate
Prepare the Royal Icing and use a cocktail stick/toothpick to add enough black food colouring paste to create a dark shade. Transfer to a small piping/pastry bag for icing and snip off the end to create a small hole. Pipe 3 lines across each macaron, as well as eyes and a tail. Leave to dry for 1 hour.

Here's an irresistible idea for the child in all of us! You can make these cute
little rabbits for a family Easter celebration or simply as a fun treat for a
spring birthday party.

bunnies

For the macaron shells

1 quantity Basic Macarons (see recipe, page 11)

3 g/⅔ teaspoon autumn leaf food colouring paste

For the filling

3 tablespoons strawberry jam/jelly

1 batch Buttercream.
(see recipe, page 24)

To decorate

20 g/¾ oz. white sugarpaste/fondant

baby pink food colouring paste

orange food colouring paste

edible gold lustre paint

1 quantity Royal Icing (see recipe, page 29)

black food colouring paste

brown food colouring paste

red nonpareils or tiny red sprinkles

2 disposable piping/pastry bags
fitted with 1-cm/½-in. round
nozzles/tips

5-cm/2-in. round template
(see page 138)

small paintbrush

2 small disposable piping/pastry bags
for icing

tiny flower cutters

Makes 40

Preheat the oven to 160°C (325°F) Gas 3.

Prepare the Basic Macarons according to the recipe on page 11, but add the autumn leaf food colouring paste before folding the egg whites into the dry ingredients. Put the mixture into a piping/pastry bag fitted with a 1-cm/½-in. round nozzle/tip.

Place the 5-cm/2-in. round template on a baking sheet, and place a transparent silicone mat on top. Pipe 40 rounds, using the template as a guide. (You will need more than one baking sheet.) Add ears to 20 of the rounds – start piping the ears from the top, and drag the nozzle/tip towards the face. Tap the bottom of the sheets lightly on the work surface to settle the mixture. Carefully slide the template out from under the silicone mat. Leave the macarons to rest for 15–30 minutes.

Bake the macarons, one sheet at a time, on the middle shelf of the preheated oven for 8 minutes, until the tops are crisp and the undersides of the macarons are dry. Leave to cool for 30 minutes on the baking sheet. Leave the oven on.

For the filling, mix the jam/jelly into the Buttercream.

Put the Buttercream into a piping/pastry bag fitted with a 1-cm/½-in. round nozzle/tip. Pipe a little filling onto the flat-sides of all the round macarons, and top with the bunny faces, pressing together gently. Leave to set in the refrigerator for at least 12 hours before serving.

To decorate

Divide the sugarpaste/fondant into two portions. Knead baby pink food colouring paste into one portion and orange food colouring paste into the other portion. Roll out both colours and use a tiny cutter to cut out tiny flower shapes. Leave to dry before use.

Use a small paintbrush to paint a stroke of gold lustre paint down the centre of all the ears.

Prepare the Royal Icing, and place one-third of the mixture into a separate bowl. Use a cocktail stick/toothpick to add black food colouring paste to the small portion and brown food colouring paste to the large portion. Transfer both portions to small piping/pastry bags for icing and snip off the ends to create small holes.

Pipe black eyes and brown whiskers onto each bunny face. Use the brown icing to pipe a small blob on each bunny's nose and at the base of its right ear. Stick some red nonpareils or sprinkles onto each nose, and a sugarpaste/fondant flower onto the base of each right ear. Leave to dry for 1 hour.

Here I use a clever stacking effect to create an unmistakable black and white panda. It is very simple but extremely effective, and can be used for other animals too, if you use your imagination!

pandas

FOR THE MACARON SHELLS
2 batches Basic Macarons (see recipe, page 11)

5 g/1 teaspoon black food colouring paste

FOR THE FILLING
1 batch Buttercream (see recipe, page 24)

3 tablespoons lemon curd

FOR THE DECORATION
1 batch Royal Icing (see recipe, page 29)

black food colouring paste

2 disposable piping/pastry bags fitted with 1-cm/½-in. round nozzles/tips

5-cm/2-in. round template (see page 138)

small disposable piping/pastry bag for icing

MAKES 40

Preheat the oven to 160°C (325°F) Gas 3.

Prepare the first batch of Basic Macarons according to the recipe on page 11. No food colouring is added to this batch. Put the mixture into a piping/pastry bag fitted with a 1-cm/½-in. round nozzle/tip.

Place the 5-cm/2-in. round template on a baking sheet, and place a transparent silicone mat on top. Pipe 40 rounds, using the template as a guide. (You will need more than one baking sheet.) Tap the bottom of the sheets lightly on the work surface to settle the mixture. Carefully slide the template out from under the silicone mat. Leave the macarons to rest for 15–30 minutes.

Bake the macarons, one sheet at a time, on the middle shelf of the preheated oven for 8 minutes, until the tops are crisp and the undersides of the macarons are dry. Leave to cool for 30 minutes on the baking sheet. Leave the oven on.

Meanwhile, prepare the second batch of Basic Macarons according to the recipe on page 11, but add the black food colouring paste before folding the egg whites into the dry ingredients. Put the mixture into a piping/pastry bag fitted with a 1-cm/½-in. round nozzle/tip.

Place the 5-cm/2-in. round template on a baking sheet, and place a transparent silicone mat on top. Pipe 80 rounds, using the template as a guide. (You will need more than one baking sheet.) Tap the bottom of the sheets lightly on the work surface to settle the mixture. Carefully slide the template out from under the silicone mat. Leave the macarons to rest for 15–30 minutes.

Bake the macarons, one sheet at a time, on the middle shelf of the preheated oven for 8 minutes, until the tops are crisp and the undersides of the macarons are dry. Leave to cool for 30 minutes on the baking sheet. These will be the pandas' bodies.

To make the filling, mix the lemon curd into the Buttercream.

Spread a teaspoonful of the filling mixture onto the flat-sides of half of the black shells, and top with the remaining black macaron shells, pressing together gently. These are the bodies. Leave to set in the refrigerator for at least 12 hours before serving.

To decorate

Make the Royal Icing recipe and use a cocktail stick/toothpick to add enough black colouring paste to make a dark shade. Transfer to a small piping/pastry bag for icing. Pipe black eyes, noses and ears onto the reserved white macaron shells. Leave to dry for 20 minutes.

Use the remaining icing to stick a face onto the top of each panda's body. Leave to dry for 1 hour.

fun food

Put together different shapes of macaron to create this inspired breakfast collection. This is really simple to create and the finished effect will put a smile on anybody's face.

egg & beans

FOR THE MACARON SHELLS

3 batches Basic Macarons (see recipe, page 11)

4 g/¾ teaspoon buttercup yellow food colouring paste

3 g/⅔ teaspoon dark tangerine orange food colouring paste

0.5 g/scant ⅛ teaspoon red food colouring paste

TO DECORATE

1 batch Royal Icing (see recipe page 29)

cocoa powder, for dusting

black pepper, to decorate

2 disposable piping/pastry bags fitted with 8-mm/⅜-in. nozzles/tips

Toast template (see page 139)

transparent silicone mat

4.5-cm/1¾-in. round template (see page 138)

2.5-cm/1-in. round template (see page 138)

disposable piping/pastry bag fitted with a 4-mm/⅛-in. nozzle/tip

Baked Beans template (see page 138)

MAKES 10

Preheat the oven to 160°C (325°F) Gas 3.

Prepare the first batch of Basic Macarons according to the recipe on page 11. No food colouring is added to this batch. Put the mixture into a piping/pastry bag fitted with an 8-mm/⅜-in. round nozzle/tip.

Place the Toast template on a baking sheet, and place a transparent silicone mat on top. Pipe the outline of the square, using the template as a guide, then fill the square carefully with the macaron mixture. Repeat to make 10 squares. Place the 4.5-cm/1¾-in. round template on a separate baking sheet, and place a transparent silicone mat on top. Using the same mixture, pipe 20 rounds onto the silicone mat. Tap the bottom of the sheets lightly on the work surface to settle the mixture. Leave the macarons to rest for 15–30 minutes.

Tap the bottom of the sheets lightly on the work surface to settle the mixture. Carefully slide the template out from under the silicone mat. Leave the macarons to rest for 15–30 minutes.

Bake the macarons, one sheet at a time, on the middle shelf of the preheated oven for 8 minutes, until the tops are crisp and the undersides of the macarons are dry. Leave to cool for 30 minutes on the baking sheet. Leave the oven on.

Prepare the second batch of Basic Macarons according to the recipe on page 11, but add the yellow food colouring paste before folding the egg whites into the dry ingredients. Put the mixture into a piping/pastry bag fitted with an 8-mm/⅛-in. round nozzle/tip.

Place the 2.5-cm/1-in. round template on a baking sheet, and place a transparent silicone mat on top. Pipe 20 rounds, using the template as a guide. Tap the bottom of the sheets lightly on the work surface to settle the mixture. Carefully slide the template out from under the mat. Leave the macarons to rest for 15–30 minutes.

Bake the macarons, one sheet at a time, on the middle shelf of the preheated oven for 6 minutes until the tops are crisp and the undersides of the macarons are dry.

Prepare the third batch of Basic Macarons according to the recipe on page 11, but add the dark tangerine and red colouring pastes before folding the egg whites into the dry ingredients. Put the mixture into a piping/pastry bag fitted with a 4-mm/⅛-in. round nozzle/tip.

Place the Baked Beans template on a baking sheet, and place a transparent silicone mat on top. Pipe beans, using the template as a guide, until you have used all the mixture. Tap the bottom of the sheets lightly on the work surface to settle the mixture. Leave the macarons to rest for 15–30 minutes.

Bake the macarons, one sheet at a time, on the middle shelf of the preheated oven for 4 minutes until the tops are crisp and the undersides of the macarons are dry.

Place a wire rack over the toast and lightly dust cocoa powder over the top. Use some Royal Icing to stick the egg yolk onto the white. Serve, sprinkled with pepper.

These macaron burger buns look very realistic thanks to the sesame seeds on top. You will need to slice your cheese into squares no larger than 7.5 cm/3 in. and the same goes for the lettuce leaves.

burger

FOR THE MACARON SHELLS
1 batch Basic Macarons (see recipe, page 11)

20 g/¾ oz. sesame seeds

FOR THE FILLING
2 beef tomatoes, cut into 25 slices

25 small lettuce leaves

25 small cheese slices

disposable piping/pastry bag fitted with a 1-cm/½-in. round nozzle/tip

6-cm/2⅜-in. round template (see page 138)

transparent silicone mat

MAKES 25

Preheat the oven to 160°C (325°F) Gas 3.

Prepare the Basic Macarons according to the recipe on page 11, adding no food colouring paste. Put the mixture into a piping/pastry bag fitted with a 1-cm/½-in. round nozzle/tip.

Place the 6-cm/2⅜-in. round template on a baking sheet, and place a transparent silicone mat on top. Pipe 50 rounds, using the template as a guide. (You will need more than one baking sheet.) Tap the bottom of the sheets lightly on the work surface to settle the mixture. Sprinkle the sesame seeds on top. Carefully slide the template out from under the silicone mat. Leave the macarons to rest for 15–30 minutes.

Bake the macarons, one sheet at a time, on the middle shelf of the preheated oven for 10 minutes until the tops are crisp and the undersides of the macarons are dry.

Lay cheese slices on half of the macaron shells, then add the lettuce slices and, lastly, the tomato. Top with another macaron shell. Serve.

You can make these tomatoes in different sizes – just remember to adjust the baking time accordingly. You could even try some green or orange tomatoes, if you like.

tomatoes

FOR THE MACARON SHELLS
1 batch Basic Macarons (see recipe, page 11)

5 g/1 teaspoon cherry red food colouring paste

FOR THE FILLING
1 batch Buttercream (see recipe, page 24)

3 tablespoons onion marmalade

FOR THE DECORATION
30 g/1 oz sugarpaste/fondant

2.5 g/½ teaspoon holly green food colouring paste

disposable piping/pastry bag fitted with a 1-cm/½-in. round nozzle/tip

5-cm/2-in. round template (see page 138)

transparent silicone mat

4-cm/1½-in. round template (see page 138)

2.5-cm/1-in. round template (see page 138)

disposable piping/pastry bag fitted with a 4-mm/⅛-in. round nozzle/tip

MAKES 30

Preheat the oven to 160°C (325°F) Gas 3.

Prepare the Basic Macarons according to the recipe on page 11, but add the cherry red food colouring paste before folding the egg whites into the dry ingredients. Put the mixture into a piping/pastry bag fitted with a 1-cm/½-in. round nozzle/tip.

Place the 5-cm/2-in. round template on a baking sheet, and place a transparent silicone mat on top. Pipe 20 rounds, using the template as a guide.

Place the 4-cm/1½-in. round template on a baking sheet, and place a transparent silicone mat on top. Pipe 20 rounds, using the template as a guide.

Place the 2.5-cm/1-in. round template on a baking sheet, and place a transparent silicone mat on top. Pipe 20 rounds, using the template as a guide.

Tap the bottom of the sheets lightly on the work surface to settle the mixture. Carefully slide the template out from under the silicone mat. Leave the macarons to rest for 15–30 minutes.

Bake the macarons, one sheet at a time, on the middle shelf of the preheated oven, until the tops are crisp and the undersides of the macarons are dry. The 5-cm/2-in. macarons will need 8 minutes, the 4-cm/1½-in. macarons will need 7 minutes, and the 2.5-cm/1-in. macarons will need 6 minutes.

Line the macarons into rows of two in their respective sizes, flat-side up. Put the Buttercream into a piping/pastry bag fitted with a 4-mm/⅛-in nozzle/tip.

Place a small blob of onion marmalade onto the base of one macaron in each pair. Pipe a thin layer of Buttercream round the edge of the onion marmalade, then sandwich the macaron pairs together gently. Leave to set in the refrigerator for at least 12 hours before serving.

To decorate
Knead the green food colouring paste into the white sugarpaste until it is evenly mixed. Use the sugarpaste to make green stalks for the tomatoes, and stick one on top of each macaron. Leave to dry for 1 hour.

Another savoury filling is used in these cute bagel macarons. Cream cheese and smoked salmon is my favourite bagel filling, but you could use a sweet filling, such as jam and Buttercream, if you prefer.

bagel

FOR THE MACARON SHELLS
1 batch Basic Macarons (see recipe, page 11)

2 g/scant ½ teaspoon dark brown food colouring paste

FOR THE FILLING
25 tiny slices smoked salmon

100 g/½ cup full-fat cream cheese

salt and ground black pepper

disposable piping/pastry bag fitted with a 1-cm/½-in. round nozzle/tip

3-cm/1¼-in. round template (see page 138)

4.5-cm/1¾-in. round template (see page 138)

transparent silicone mat

MAKES 25

Preheat the oven to 160°C (325°F) Gas 3.

Prepare the Basic Macarons according to the recipe on page 11, but add the dark brown food colouring paste before folding the egg whites into the dry ingredients. Put the mixture into a piping/pastry bag fitted with a 1-cm/½-in. round nozzle/tip.

Create a bagel template by using the 3-cm/1¼-in. round template inside the 4.5-cm/1¾-in. round template. Place the template on a baking sheet and place a transparent silicone mat on top. Pipe 50 rings, using the template as a guide. Tap the bottom of the sheets lightly on the work surface to settle the mixture. Carefully slide the template out from under the silicone mat. Leave the macarons to rest for 15–30 minutes.

Bake the macarons, one sheet at a time, on the middle shelf of the preheated oven for 8 minutes, until the tops are crisp and the undersides of the macarons are dry. Leave to cool for 30 minutes on the baking sheets.

Spread the cream cheese on half of the macaron shells, then add the smoked salmon slices. Season with salt and pepper, and top with the remaining macaron shells. Serve.

These swirly macaron pops are a lovely idea to serve at parties – they are popular with children and adults alike. Make sure the sticks are suitable for food use and avoid those with pointy ends.

lollipops

FOR THE MACARON SHELLS

3 batches Basic Macarons (see recipe, page 11)

3 g/²⁄₃ teaspoon lime green food colouring paste

5 g/1 teaspoon Christmas red food colouring paste

FOR THE FILLINGS

1 batch Chocolate Ganache (see recipe, page 23)

50 g/¼ cup dried passionfruit

1 batch Buttercream (see recipe, page 24)

2–3 drops bubble gum essence oil

50 g/¼ cup dried red berries

2 disposable piping/pastry bags fitted with 1-cm/½-in. round nozzles/tips

7-cm/2¾-in. round template (see page 138)

transparent silicone mat

14 lollipop sticks

MAKES 14

Prepare the first batch of Basic Macarons according to the recipe on page 11. No food colouring is added to this batch.

Prepare the second batch of Basic Macarons according to the recipe on page 11, but add the lime green food colouring paste before folding the egg whites into the dry ingredients.

Prepare the third batch of Basic Macarons according to the recipe on page 11, but add the Christmas red food colouring paste before folding the egg whites into the dry ingredients.

Put half of the white macaron mixture down one side of a piping/pastry bag fitted with a 1-cm/½-in. round nozzle/tip, then add the green mixture down the other side of the bag, so that you will get a bit of both colours when piped.

Put the other half of the white macaron mixture down one side of a piping/pastry bag fitted with a 1-cm/½-in. round nozzle/tip, then add the red mixture down the other side of the bag, so that you will get a bit of both colours when piped.

Place the 7-cm/2¾-in. round template on a baking sheet, and place a transparent silicone mat on top. Starting from the outside, and leaving 1-mm/¹⁄₁₆-in. between the lines to allow for expansion, pipe 14 green spirals and 14 red spirals within the round templates. (You will need more than one baking sheet.) Tap the bottom of the sheets lightly on the work surface to settle the mixture. Carefully slide the template out from under the silicone mat. Leave the macarons to rest for 15–30 minutes.

Bake the macarons, one sheet at a time, on the middle shelf of the preheated oven for 12 minutes, until the tops are crisp and the undersides of the macarons are dry. Leave to cool for 30 minutes on the baking sheet.

To make the fillings, prepare the Chocolate Ganache and mix in the dried passionfruit. Prepare the Buttercream, and mix in the bubble gum essence oil and dried berries.

Line the macaron shells in pairs of the same colour, flat-side up. Using a teaspoon, place a little Chocolate Ganache mixture onto half of the red macaron shells, add a lollipop stick, then sandwich the pairs together gently. Repeat with the green macaron shells, filling them with the Buttercream. Leave to set in the refrigerator for at least 12 hours before serving.

pretty in pink

These beautiful heart-shaped macarons in shades of red, pink and lilac and painted with a delicate gold lustre, make the perfect treat for Valentine's Day or a special treat for any loved one, any day of the year!

love hearts

FOR THE MACARON SHELLS
3 batches Basic Macarons (see recipe, page 11)

2.5 g/½ teaspoon dusky pink food colouring paste

3 g/⅔ teaspoon pink food colouring paste

2.5 g/½ teaspoon claret food colouring paste

FOR THE FILLING
a few drops of rose cordial

1 batch Buttercream (see recipe, page 24)

FOR THE DECORATION
30 g/1 oz white sugarpaste/fondant

purple food colouring paste

egg yellow food colouring paste

pink food colouring paste

1 batch Royal Icing (see recipe, page 29)

3 disposable piping/pastry bags fitted with 8-mm/⅜-in. round nozzles/tips

Heart template

transparent silicone mat

small disposable piping/pastry bag for icing

mini flower cutters

MAKES 120

Preheat the oven to 160°C (325°F) Gas 3.

Prepare the first batch of Basic Macarons according to the recipe on page 11, but add the dusky pink food colouring paste in step 4 before folding the egg whites into the dry ingredients. Put the mixture into a piping/pastry bag fitted with an 8-mm/⅜-in nozzle/tip.

Place the Heart template on a baking sheet, and place a transparent silicone mat on top. Pipe 80 hearts, using the template as a guide. (You will need more than one baking sheet.) Tap the bottom of the sheets lightly on the work surface to settle the mixture. Carefully slide the template out from under the silicone mat. Leave the macarons to rest for 15–30 minutes.

Bake the macarons, one sheet at a time, on the middle shelf of the preheated oven for 8 minutes, until the tops are crisp and the undersides of the macarons are dry. Leave to cool for 30 minutes on the baking sheet. Leave the oven on.

Repeat this process with the second and third batch of Basic Macarons, using the pink food colouring paste in one batch and the claret food colouring paste in the other.

For the filling, mix the rose cordial into the Buttercream.

Line the macarons in pairs of the same colour (or mix and match, if you like).

Fill one half of the shells with Buttercream, then sandwich the macarons together gently. Leave to set in the refrigerator for at least 12 hours before serving.

To decorate
Divide the sugarpaste/fondant into thirds. Use a cocktail stick/ toothpick to add some purple food colouring paste to one portion, egg yellow food colouring paste to one portion, and pink food colouring paste to the final portion. Knead each portion until the colour is even. Roll out the coloured icing and use the little flower cutter to cut out flowers in the three colours. Leave to dry before use.

Make the Royal Icing recipe and divide it into two portions. Use a cocktail stick/ toothpick to add some purple food colouring paste to one portion and red food colouring paste to the other portion. Transfer to two small piping/pastry bags for icing, and snip off the ends to create small holes. Pipe decorative dots onto the macaron hearts, then use the icing to stick the little flowers onto the macarons. Leave to dry for 1 hour.

Variations
For alternative fillings, try a few tablespoons of strawberry jam/jelly mixed into Buttercream, or some raspberry jam mixed into a Chocolate Ganache.

These elegant and chic macarons make a delightful addition to an afternoon tea selection. You can top these with fresh rose petals, but make sure the petals are suitable for eating first.

rose petals

FOR THE MACARON SHELLS
2 batches Basic Macarons (see recipe, page 11)

5 g/1 teaspoon rose pink food colouring paste

FOR THE FILLING
3 tablespoons seedless raspberry jam/jelly

1 quantity Buttercream (see recipe, page 24)

a few drops rose cordial, to taste

TO DECORATE
fresh edible rose petals or crystallized rose petals

2 disposable piping/pastry bags fitted with 1-cm/½-in. round nozzles/tips

transparent silicone mat

5-cm/2-in round template (see page 138)

MAKES 40

Preheat the oven to 160°C (325°F) Gas 3.

Prepare the Basic Macarons according to the recipe on page 11, but add the rose pink food colouring paste before folding the egg whites into the dry ingredients. Put the mixture into a piping/pastry bag fitted with a 1-cm/½-in. round nozzle/tip.

Place the 5-cm/2-in. round template on a baking sheet, and place a transparent silicone mat on top. Pipe 80 rounds, using the template as a guide. (You will need more than one baking sheet.) Tap the bottom of the sheets lightly on the work surface to settle the mixture. Carefully slide the template out from under the silicone mat. Leave the macarons to rest for 15–30 minutes.

Bake the macarons, one sheet at a time, on the middle shelf of the preheated oven for 8 minutes, until the tops are crisp and the undersides of the macarons are dry. Leave to cool for 30 minutes on the baking sheet.

To make the filling, mix the jam/jelly into the Buttercream and add the rose cordial to taste.

Spread a teaspoonful of the filling mixture onto the flat-sides of half of the shells, and top with the remaining macaron shells, pressing together gently. Leave to set in the refrigerator for at least 12 hours before serving.

To decorate
Decorate with rose petals, using a dot of Buttercream to attach them.

These stunning creations make a special dessert for a dinner party. You can make the macaron shells in advance, then you will just need to assemble them before serving to impressed dinner guests!

raspberry sandwich

FOR THE MACARON SHELLS
2 batches Basic Macarons (see recipe, page 11)

2.5 g/½ teaspoon rose pink food colouring paste

3 g/⅔ teaspoon baby pink food colouring paste

FOR THE FILLING
20 tablespoons ice cream or clotted cream

about 200 fresh raspberries

TO DECORATE
fresh edible rose petals or crystallized rose petals

2 disposable piping/pastry bags fitted with 1-cm/½-in. round nozzles/tips

6-cm/2⅜-in. round template (see page 138)

transparent silicone mat

7-cm/2¾-in. round template (see page 138)

MAKES 20

Preheat the oven to 160°C (325°F) Gas 3.

Prepare the Basic Macarons according to the recipe on page 11, but add the rose pink food colouring paste before folding the egg whites into the dry ingredients. Put the mixture into a piping/pastry bag fitted with a 1-cm/½-in. round nozzle/tip.

Place the 6-cm/2⅜-in. round template on a baking sheet, and place a transparent silicone mat on top. Pipe 20 rounds, using the template as a guide. (You will need more than one baking sheet.) Tap the bottom of the sheets lightly on the work surface to settle the mixture. Carefully slide the template out from under the silicone mat. Leave the macarons to rest for 15–30 minutes.

Bake the macarons, one sheet at a time, on the middle shelf of the preheated oven for 9 minutes until the tops are crisp and the undersides of the macarons are dry.

Prepare the second batch of Basic Macarons according to the recipe on page 11, but add the baby pink food colouring paste before folding the egg whites into the dry ingredients. Put the mixture into a piping/pastry bag fitted with a 1-cm/½-in. round nozzle/tip.

Place the 7-cm/2¾-in. round template on a baking sheet, and place a transparent silicone mat on top. Pipe 20 rounds, using the template as a guide. (You will need more than one baking sheet.) Tap the bottom of the sheets lightly on the work surface to settle the mixture. Carefully slide the template out from under the silicone mat. Leave the macarons to rest for 15–30 minutes.

Bake the macarons, one sheet at a time, on the middle shelf of the preheated oven for 10 minutes until the tops are crisp and the undersides of the macarons are dry.

When you are ready to serve, place the larger macaron shells on serving plates, flat-side down, and top each one with a tablespoonful of ice cream or clotted cream. Arrange fresh raspberries around the edge, then top with a smaller macaron shell, flat-side down.

To decorate
Decorate with rose petals.

The delicate beauty of cherry blossoms is captured in these divine macarons. They are filled with a sakura-scented Buttercream and hand-painted with pretty flowers.

sakura cherry blossom

FOR THE MACARON SHELLS
1 batch Basic Macarons (see recipe, page 11)

3 g/⅔ teaspoon dusky pink food colouring paste

FOR THE FILLING
1 batch Buttercream (see recipe, page 24)

edible sakura paste or other edible flower paste, to taste

TO DECORATE
2.5 g/½ teaspoon brown food colouring paste

2.5 g/½ teaspoon pink food colouring paste

2.5 g/½ teaspoon white food colouring paste

rejuvenating spirit to dilute the food colouring pastes

disposable piping/pastry bag fitted with a 1-cm/½-in. round nozzle/tip

5-cm/2-in. round template (see page 138)

transparent silicone mat

fine paintbrush

MAKES 40

Preheat the oven to 160°C (325°F) Gas 3.

Prepare the Basic Macarons according to the recipe on page 11, but add the dusky pink food colouring paste before folding the egg whites into the dry ingredients. Put the mixture into a piping/pastry bag fitted with a 1-cm/½-in. round nozzle/tip.

Place the 5-cm/2-in. round template on a baking sheet, and place a transparent silicone mat on top. Pipe 80 rounds, using the template as a guide. (You will need more than one baking sheet.) Tap the bottom of the sheets lightly on the work surface to settle the mixture. Carefully slide the template out from under the silicone mat. Leave the macarons to rest for 15–30 minutes.

Bake the macarons, one sheet at a time, on the middle shelf of the preheated oven for 8 minutes, until the tops are crisp and the undersides of the macarons are dry. Leave to cool for 30 minutes on the baking sheet.

For the filling, mix the edible sakura flower paste into the Buttercream.

Spread a teaspoonful of the filling mixture onto the flat-sides of half of the shells, and top with the remaining macaron shells, pressing together gently. Leave to set in the refrigerator for at least 12 hours before serving.

To decorate
Dilute the food colouring pastes using the rejuvenating spirit, and use a clean, fine paintbrush to paint branches and flowers onto the tops of the macarons. Leave to dry for 1 hour.

This bouquet of macaron flowers makes an ideal gift for Mother's Day. Paint them with your favourite flowers, using whatever colours you like. You will need both a flat and a fine paintbrush to achieve the effects shown here.

hand-painted bouquet

For the macaron shells

2 batches Basic Macarons (see recipe, page 11)

2.5 g/½ teaspoon pink food colouring paste

3 g/⅔ teaspoon gooseberry food colouring paste

For the filling

3 tablespoons rose cordial

1 batch White Chocolate Ganache (see recipe, page 23)

2 teaspoons green tea powder

1 batch Buttercream (see recipe, page 24)

7 tablespoons red bean paste (available from large supermarkets and Chinese stores)

To decorate

2.5 g/½ teaspoon red food colouring paste

2.5 g/½ teaspoon green food colouring paste

2.5 g/½ teaspoon yellow food colouring paste

rejuvenating spirit to dilute the food colouring pastes

2 disposable piping/pastry bags fitted with 1-cm/½-in. round nozzles/tips

5.5-cm/2¼-in. round template (see page 138)

transparent silicone mat

4-cm/1½-in. round template (see page 138)

flat and fine paintbrushes

Makes 40

Preheat the oven to 160°C (325°F) Gas 3.

Prepare the first batch of Basic Macarons according to the recipe on page 11, but add the pink food colouring paste before folding the egg whites into the dry ingredients. Put the mixture into a piping/pastry bag fitted with a 1-cm/½-in. round nozzle/tip.

Place the 5.5-cm/2¼-in. round template on a baking sheet, and place a transparent silicone mat on top. Pipe 40 rounds, using the template as a guide. (You will need more than one baking sheet.) Tap the bottom of the sheets lightly on the work surface to settle the mixture. Carefully slide the template out from under the silicone mat. Leave the macarons to rest for 15–30 minutes.

Bake the macarons, one sheet at a time, on the middle shelf of the preheated oven for 8 minutes, until the tops are crisp and the undersides of the macarons are dry. Leave to cool for 30 minutes on the baking sheet. Leave the oven on.

Meanwhile, prepare the second batch of Basic Macarons according to the recipe on page 11, but add the gooseberry food colouring paste before folding the egg whites into the dry ingredients. Put the mixture into a piping/pastry bag fitted with a 1-cm/½-in. round nozzle/tip.

Place the 4-cm/1½-in. round template on a baking sheet, and place a transparent silicone mat on top. Pipe 60 rounds, using the template as a guide. (You will need more than one baking sheet.) Tap the bottom of the sheets lightly on the work surface to settle the mixture. Carefully slide the template out from under the silicone mat. Leave the macarons to rest for 15–30 minutes.

Bake the macarons, one sheet at a time, on the middle shelf of the preheated oven for 8 minutes, until the tops are crisp and the undersides of the macarons are dry. Leave to cool for 30 minutes on the baking sheet.

For the fillings, mix the rose cordial into the White Chocolate Ganache and the green tea powder into the Buttercream.

Arrange the macaron shells in pairs of the same colour. Place a teaspoonful of White Chocolate Ganache onto the flat-side of half of the pink macarons and top with the remaining pink macarons, pressing them together gently. Place half a teaspoonful of red bean paste onto the flat-side of half of the green macarons, leaving a thin gap around the edge. Use a piping/pastry bag fitted with a 4-mm/⅛-in. nozzle to pipe a ring of Buttercream around the edge of the red bean paste. Leave to set in the refrigerator for at least 12 hours before serving.

To decorate

Dilute the food colouring pastes with a little rejuvenating spirit, and use a clean, flat paintbrush to paint flowers onto the tops of the macarons. Use a fine paintbrush to paint stems and detail. Leave to dry for 1 hour.

Here is how to really achieve the wow factor with your macarons. All you need is a polystyrene ball and plenty of cocktail sticks/ toothpicks to hold the macarons in place.

macaron flower pot

FOR THE MACARONS

3 batches Basic Macarons (see recipe, page 11)

2.5 g/½ teaspoon dusky pink food colouring paste

3 g/⅔ teaspoon pink food colouring paste

2.5 g/½ teaspoon claret food colouring paste

FOR THE FILLING

3 batches Buttercream (see recipe, page 24)

3 tablespoons strawberry jam/jelly

3 tablespoons raspberry jam/jelly

a few drops rose cordial, to taste

TO DECORATE

2.5 g/½ teaspoon purple food colouring paste

20 g/¾ oz. sugarpaste/fondant

2 batches Royal Icing (see recipe, page 29)

edible sugar pearls

3 disposable piping/pastry bags fitted with 8-mm/⅜-in. round nozzles/tips

2.5-cm/1-in. round template (see page 138)

transparent silicone mat

small disposable piping/pastry bag for icing

tiny flower cutters

12-cm/4¾-in. polystyrene ball

1 flat paint brush

cocktail sticks/toothpicks

MAKES 120

Preheat the oven to 160°C (325°F) Gas 3.

Prepare the first batch of Basic Macarons according to the recipe on page 11, but add the dusky pink food colouring paste before folding the egg whites into the dry ingredients. Put the mixture into a piping/pastry bag fitted with a 1-cm/½-in. round nozzle/tip.

Place the 2.5-cm/1-in. round template on a baking sheet, and place a transparent silicone mat on top. Pipe 80 rounds, using the template as a guide. (You will need more than one baking sheet.) Tap the bottom of the sheets lightly on the work surface to settle the mixture. Carefully slide the template out from under the silicone mat. Leave the macarons to rest for 15–30 minutes.

Bake the macarons, one sheet at a time, on the middle shelf of the preheated oven for 6 minutes, until the tops are crisp and the undersides of the macarons are dry. Leave to cool for 30 minutes on the baking sheet. Leave the oven on.

Repeat the process with the second and third batches of Basic Macarons, adding the pink food colouring paste to the second batch and the claret food colouring paste to the third batch.

To make the fillings, mix the strawberry jam/jelly into one batch of Buttercream, mix the raspberry jam/jelly into the second batch of Buttercream, and mix the rose cordial into the third batch of Buttercream.

Line the macaron shells into pairs of the same colour. Fill the dusky pink macarons with a teaspoonful of strawberry Buttercream and sandwich together gently. Fill the pink macarons with a teaspoonful of raspberry Buttercream and sandwich together gently. Fill the claret macarons with a teaspoonful of rose Buttercream and sandwich together gently. Leave to set in the refrigerator for at least 12 hours before serving.

Knead the purple food colouring paste into the sugarpaste/fondant until it is evenly mixed. Roll out thinly and use the cutter to cut the flowers. Shape them between your fingers to make them into flower shapes. Leave to dry before use.

Prepare a double batch of Royal Icing and spread half of it over the polystyrene ball using a flat paintbrush. Put the remaining icing into a small piping/pastry bag for icing and pipe tiny dots in the middle of the flowers, then stick an edible sugar pearl onto each one. Leave to dry for 20 minutes.

Push a cocktail stick/toothpick into a macaron, making sure that it does not go all the way through. Carefully push the other end of the cocktail stick/toothpick into the polystyrene ball, making sure it is secure. Repeat with the rest of the macarons, arranging them around the ball so that they are evenly spaced. Use the Royal Icing to stick the sugar flowers between the macarons. Leave to dry for 1 hour.

Canned lychees are perfect for using in the filling as they are available to buy in most large supermarkets. The little painted lychees on the tops stand out wonderfully against the white shell.

lychee bites

FOR THE MACARON SHELLS
2 batches Basic Macarons (see recipe, page 11)

3 g/²⁄₃ teaspoon baby pink food colouring paste

FOR THE FILLING
a few drops rose cordial, to taste

200 g/generous ½ cup raspberry jam/jelly

400-g/14-oz. can lychees in syrup, drained and chopped

TO DECORATE
2.5 g/½ teaspoon pink food colouring paste

2.5 g/½ teaspoon green food colouring paste

rejuvenating spirit to dilute the food colouring pastes

transparent silicone mat

5-cm/2-in. round templates (see page 138)

2 disposable piping/pastry bags fitted with 1-cm/½-in. round nozzles/tips

2 fine paintbrushes

MAKES 40

Preheat the oven to 160°C (325°F) Gas 3.

Prepare the first batch of Basic Macarons according to the recipe on page 11. No food colouring is added to this batch. Put the mixture into a piping/pastry bag fitted with a 1-cm/½-in. round nozzle/tip.

Place the 5-cm/2-in. round template on a baking sheet, and place a transparent silicone mat on top. Pipe 40 rounds onto the silicone mat, using the template as a guide. (You will need more than one baking sheet.) Tap the bottom of the sheets lightly on the work surface to settle the mixture. Carefully slide the template out from under the silicone mat. Leave the macarons to rest for 15–30 minutes.

Bake the macarons, one sheet at a time, on the middle shelf of the preheated oven for 8 minutes, until the tops are crisp and the undersides of the macarons are dry. Leave to cool for 30 minutes on the baking sheet. Leave the oven on.

Meanwhile, prepare the second batch of Basic Macarons according to the recipe on page 11, but add the baby pink food colouring paste before folding the egg whites into the dry ingredients. Put the mixture into a piping/pastry bag fitted with a 1-cm/½-in. round nozzle/tip.

Place the 5-cm/2-in. round template on a baking sheet, and place a transparent silicone mat on top. Pipe 40 rounds, using the template as a guide. (You will need more than one baking sheet.) Tap the bottom of the sheets lightly on the work surface to settle the mixture. Carefully slide the template out from under the silicone mat. Leave the macarons to rest for 15–30 minutes.

Bake the macarons, one sheet at a time, on the middle shelf of the preheated oven for 8 minutes, until the tops are crisp and the undersides of the macarons are dry. Leave to cool for 30 minutes on the baking sheet.

To make the filling, add the rose cordial to the raspberry jam/jelly, then mix in the chopped lychees.

Spread a teaspoonful of the filling mixture onto the flat-sides of each pink macaron shell, then top with the white shells, and press together gently. Leave to set in the refrigerator for at least 12 hours before serving.

To decorate
Dilute the food colouring pastes using the rejuvenating spirit. Use a fine paintbrush to paint two tiny pink lychees on each white shell, then add green leaves with another paintbrush. Leave to dry for 1 hour.

precious gifts

A wonderful addition to any party decor, a sparkling crown will surprise and impress all your guests. I made a few tiny macarons to complete the crown, and dotted some orange icing in-between.

gems in crown

FOR THE MACARON SHELLS
1 batch Basic Macarons
(see recipe, page 11)

3 g/²⁄₃ teaspoon autumn leaf food colouring paste

FOR THE FILLING
1 batch Caramel Chocolate Ganache (see recipe, page 24)

TO DECORATE
1 batch Royal Icing (see recipe, page 29)

autumn leaf food colouring paste

40 1-cm/½-in. sugar diamond stones

1 small can of edible gold lustre shimmer spray

egg food colouring paste

disposable piping/pastry bag fitted with a 1-cm/½-in. round nozzle/tip

5-cm/2-in. round template
(see page 138)

transparent silicone mat

small disposable piping/pastry bag for icing

MAKES 40

Preheat the oven to 160°C (325°F) Gas 3.

Prepare the Basic Macarons according to the recipe on page 11, but add the autumn leaf food colouring paste before folding the egg whites into the dry ingredients. Put the mixture into a piping/pastry bag fitted with a 1-cm/½-in. round nozzle/tip.

Place the 5-cm/2-in. round template on a baking sheet, and place a transparent silicone mat on top. Pipe 80 round macarons onto the silicone mat, using the template as a guide. (You may need more than one baking sheet.)

Tap the bottom of the sheet lightly on the work surface to settle the mixture. Carefully slide the template out from under the silicone mat. Leave the macarons to rest for 15–30 minutes.

Bake the macarons, one sheet at a time, on the middle shelf of the preheated oven for 8 minutes, until the tops are crisp and the undersides of the macarons are dry. Leave to cool for 30 minutes on the baking sheet.

Place the macaron shells in two rows. Spread the Caramel Chocolate Ganache filling onto the flat-sides of half the shells and top with the remaining shells, pressing them together gently. Leave to set in the refrigerator for at least 12 hours before serving.

To decorate
Spray the shells with the edible gold lustre. Using a cocktail stick/toothpick and a little Royal Icing, stick a sugar diamond stone in the centre of each macaron.

Use a cocktail stick/toothpick to add a little autumn leaf food colouring paste to the remaining Royal Icing and, using the small disposable piping/pastry bag for icing, pipe tiny dots around the diamonds. Leave to dry for 1 hour.

Semi-precious stones and macarons – a combination devoutly to be wished. The peppermint gives a clean, fresh taste, which is reflected in the brilliant colour. One of these lovely macarons is eyecatching, a display is a centrepiece.

turquoise with pearls

FOR THE MACARON SHELLS
1 batch Basic Macarons
(see recipe, page 11)

3 g/⅔ teaspoon teal food
colouring paste

FOR THE FILLING
1 batch Buttercream (see recipe,
page 24)

a few drops peppermint essence
oil, to taste

TO DECORATE
1 batch Royal Icing (see recipe,
page 29)

1-cm/½-in. pink sugar diamond
stones

1 small can of edible pearl lustre
shimmer spray

20 g/¾ oz. sugar pearls

*disposable piping/pastry bag fitted
with a 1-cm/½-in. round nozzle/tip*

*5-cm/2-in. round template
(see page 138)*

transparent silicone mat

*small disposable piping/pastry bag
for icing*

MAKES 40

Preheat the oven to 160°C (325°F) Gas 3.

Prepare the Basic Macarons according to the recipe on page 11, but add the teal food colouring paste before folding the egg whites into the dry ingredients. Put the mixture into a piping/pastry bag fitted with a 1-cm/½-in. round nozzle/tip.

Place the 5-mm/¼-in. round template on a baking sheet, and place a transparent silicone mat on top. Pipe 80 macarons onto the silicone mat, using the template as a guide. (You may need more than one baking sheet.)

Tap the bottom of the sheet lightly on the work surface to settle the mixture. Carefully slide the template out from under the silicone mat. Leave the macarons to rest for 15–30 minutes.

Bake the macarons, one sheet at a time, on the middle shelf of the preheated oven for 8 minutes, until the tops are crisp and the undersides of the macarons are dry. Leave to cool for 30 minutes on the baking sheet.

For the filling, add the peppermint essence oil to the Buttercream.

Place the macaron shells in two rows. Spread the Buttercream mixture onto the flat-sides of half the shells and top with the remaining shells, pressing them together gently. Leave to set in the refrigerator for at least 12 hours before serving.

To decorate

Spray the shells with the edible pearl lustre. Using a cocktail stick/toothpick and a little Royal Icing, stick a pink sugar diamond stone in the centre of each macaron and sugar pearls around them. Leave to dry for 1 hour.

Unusual, striking, delicious! The black and gold macarons make a sophisticated addition to any table, perfectly offset by their sesame-encrusted apricot partners.

encrusted apricot

FOR THE MACARON SHELLS
2 batches Basic Macarons
(see recipe, page 11)

5 g/1 teaspoon extra black food colouring paste

3 g/²⁄₃ teaspoon tangerine food colouring paste

FOR THE FILLING
1 ready-to-eat dried apricot, finely chopped

1 batch White Chocolate Ganache (see recipe, page 23)

TO DECORATE
gold food colouring powder

rejuvenating spirit to dilute the colouring powder

1 batch Royal Icing (see recipe, page 29)

10 g/2 teaspoons mixed black and white sesame seeds

5-cm/2-in. round template
(see page 138)

transparent silicone mat

2 piping/pastry bags fitted with 1-cm/½-in. round nozzles/tips

flat paintbrush

MAKES 60

Preheat the oven to 160°C (325°F) Gas 3.

Prepare the first batch of Basic Macarons according to the recipe on page 11, but add the extra black food colouring paste before folding the egg whites into the dry ingredients. Put the mixture into a piping/pastry bag fitted with a 1-cm/½-in. round nozzle/tip,

Place the 5-cm/2-in. round template on a baking sheet, and place a transparent silicone mat on top. Pipe 60 macarons onto the silicone mat, using the template as a guide. (You may need more than one baking sheet.)

Tap the bottom of the sheet lightly on the work surface to settle the mixture. Carefully slide the template out from under the silicone mat. Leave the macarons to rest for 15–30 minutes.

Bake the macarons, one sheet at a time, on the middle shelf of the preheated oven for 8 minutes, until the tops are crisp and the undersides of the macarons are dry. Leave to cool for 30 minutes on the baking sheet. Leave the oven on.

Meanwhile, prepare the second batch of Basic Macarons according to the recipe on page 11, but add the tangerine food colouring paste before folding the egg whites into the dry ingredients. Then continue as above.

For the filling, mix the chopped dried apricot into the ganache.

Place the macaron shells in two rows, keeping the colours separate. Spread the filling onto the flat-sides of half the shells and top with the remaining shells, pressing them together gently. Leave to set in the refrigerator for at least 12 hours before serving.

To decorate
For the black macarons, add the rejuvenating spirit to the gold food colouring powder and, using the flat brush, paint the tops of the macarons with straight upward strokes.

For the apricot macarons, prepare the Royal Icing according to the recipe on page 29 and use it to stick the sesame seeds onto the macarons in clusters. Leave to dry for 1 hour.

A child's old-fashioned toy decorating an ultra-modern teatime treat – the result is a delight and children, especially, will love them. You can change colourings to suit – why not go for a multicoloured plateful?

rocking horse

FOR THE MACARON SHELLS
1 batch Basic Macarons (see recipe, page 11)

3 g/⅔ teaspoon teal food colouring paste

FOR THE FILLING
2–3 tablespoons plum conserve

1 batch Buttercream (see recipe, page 24)

TO DECORATE
500 g/3 cups white chocolate, chopped into small pieces

1 small can of edible gold lustre shimmer spray

5-cm/2-in. round template (see page 138)

transparent silicone mat

disposable piping/pastry bag fitted with a 1-cm/½-in. round nozzle/tip

chocolate thermometer

mini chocolate rocking-horse mould

MAKES 40

Preheat the oven to 160°C (325°F) Gas 3.

Prepare the Basic Macarons according to the recipe on page 11, but add the teal food colouring paste before folding the egg whites into the dry ingredients. Put the mixture into a piping/pastry bag fitted with a 1-cm/½-in. round nozzle/tip,

Place the 5-cm/2-in. round template on a baking sheet, and place a transparent silicone mat on top. Pipe 80 macarons onto the silicone mat, using the template as a guide. (You may need more than one baking sheet.)

Tap the bottom of the sheet lightly on the work surface to settle the mixture. Carefully slide the template out from under the silicone mat. Leave the macarons to rest for 15–30 minutes.

Bake the macarons, one sheet at a time, on the middle shelf of the preheated oven for 8 minutes, until the tops are crisp and the undersides of the macarons are dry. Leave to cool for 30 minutes on the baking sheet.

For the filling, mix the plum conserve into the Buttercream.

Place the macaron shells in two rows. Spread the filling onto the flat-sides of half the shells and top with the remaining shells, pressing them together gently. Leave to set in the refrigerator for at least 12 hours before serving.

To decorate

Put half of the white chocolate into a microwave-safe bowl and place in the microwave to melt, taking it out and stirring it every 15–20 seconds, until evenly melted and smooth. Stir well to ensure that the temperature of the chocolate is evenly distributed – the temperature should not be higher than about 40°C (104°F) on a chocolate thermometer.

Add half of the remaining chocolate and heat in the microwave again. Check and stir every 15–20 seconds, until smooth. Add the remaining chocolate and stir, but do not put it in the microwave this time. There will still be chocolate pieces and the temperature should be about 32°C (90°F). Keep stirring, until all the pieces of chocolate have melted and the temperature is about 29°C (84°F). The chocolate is now tempered and ready to work with. (Please note that different brands of chocolate temper at varying temperatures, so check manufacturer's instructions for precise temperatures.)

Pour the tempered white chocolate into the rocking-horse moulds. Leave to set for 2 hours before removing the rocking horses from the moulds. Spray each horse with edible gold lustre and attach one to each macaron with a little melted chocolate. Leave to dry for 1 hour.

The buttercup yellow and the mixture of lime and mint green complement each other perfectly, and no great artistic skill is necessary to paint these delicate dragonflies.

dragonfly

For the macaron shells
1 batch Basic Macarons (see recipe, page 11)

2.5 g/½ teaspoon buttercup yellow food colouring paste

For the filling
1 batch Buttercream (see recipe, page 24)

50 g/2 oz. candied melon

To decorate
1 batch Royal Icing (see recipe, page 29)

2.5g/½ teaspoon lime green food colouring paste

1.5g/¼ teaspoon mint green food colouring paste

rejuvenating spirit to dilute the colouring

5-cm/2-in. round template (see page 138)

transparent silicone mat

disposable piping/pastry bag fitted with a 1-cm/½-in. round nozzle/tip

fine paintbrush

small disposable piping/pastry bag for icing

Makes 60

Preheat the oven to 160°C (325°F) Gas 3.

Prepare the Basic Macarons according to the recipe on page 11, but add the buttercup yellow food colouring paste before folding the egg whites into the dry ingredients. Put the mixture into a piping/pastry bag fitted with a 1-cm/½-in. round nozzle/tip,

Place the 5-cm/2-in. round template on a baking sheet, and place a transparent silicone mat on top. Pipe 120 macarons onto the silicone mat, using the template as a guide. (You will need more than one baking sheet.)

Tap the bottom of the sheet lightly on the work surface to settle the mixture. Carefully slide the template out from under the silicone mat. Leave the macarons to rest for 15–30 minutes.

Bake the macarons, one sheet at a time, on the middle shelf of the preheated oven for 8 minutes, until the tops are crisp and the undersides of the macarons are dry. Leave to cool for 30 minutes on the baking sheet.

For the filling, mix the candied melon into the Buttercream.

Place the macaron shells in two rows. Spread the filling onto the flat-sides of half the shells and top with the remaining shells, pressing them together gently. Leave to set in the refrigerator for at least 12 hours before serving.

To decorate

Prepare the Royal Icing according to the recipe on page 29 and add a little of each of the food colourings. Use a small disposable piping/pastry bag to pipe three spaced dots in a curve on top of each macaron.

Dilute the rest of the two food colourings with rejuvenating spirit and use the slim brush to paint the body of the dragonfly onto each macaron, connecting the three dots and adding wings and antennae. Leave to dry for 1 hour.

These charming blue and white macarons, fresh and pretty, allow you to show your skill and creativity in cake decoration. Present your delicate lacy offerings on pure white doilies to complete the effect.

lace

FOR THE MACARON SHELLS
1 batch Basic Macarons
(see recipe, page 11)

3 g/⅔ teaspoon royal blue food colouring paste

FOR THE FILLING
1 batch Buttercream (see recipe, page 24)

2 tablespoons mango purée

20 g/¾ oz. dried mango, finely chopped

TO DECORATE
lace effect kit (see page 34)

disposable piping/pastry bag fitted with a 1-cm/½-in. round nozzle/tip

5-cm/2-in. round template (see page 138)

transparent silicone mat

MAKES 40

Preheat the oven to 160°C (325°F) Gas 3.

Prepare the Basic Macarons according to the recipe on page 11, but add the royal blue food colouring paste before folding the egg whites into the dry ingredients. Put the mixture into a piping/pastry bag fitted with a 1-cm/½-in. round nozzle/tip,

Place the 5-cm/2-in. round template on a baking sheet, and place a transparent silicone mat on top. Pipe 80 round macarons onto the silicone mat, using the template as a guide. (You may need more than one baking sheet.)

Tap the bottom of the sheet lightly on the work surface to settle the mixture. Carefully slide the template out from under the silicone mat. Leave the macarons to rest for 15–30 minutes.Carefully slide the template out from under the silicone mat. Leave the macarons to rest for 15–30 minutes.

Bake the macarons, one sheet at a time, on the middle shelf of the preheated oven for 8 minutes, until the tops are crisp and the undersides of the macarons are dry. Leave to cool for 30 minutes on the baking tray.

For the filling, combine the mango purée and dried mango into the Buttercream.

Place the macaron shells in two rows. Spread the filling onto the flat-sides of half the shells and top with the remaining shells, pressing them together gently. Leave to set in the refrigerator for at least 12 hours before serving.

To decorate
Follow the instructions for creating a sugar lace effect on page 34.

Innovative and stunning though this necklace is, it's probably best to discourage children from attempting to put it around their necks – just let them feast their eyes on it before gobbling it up.

necklace

FOR THE MACARON SHELLS
1 batch Basic Macarons (see recipe, page 11)

3.5 g/⅝ teaspoon honey gold food colouring paste

TO DECORATE
1 batch Royal Icing (see recipe, page 29)

7 white sugar diamonds (or 6 white and I pink)

64 sugar pearls

1 small can of edible pearl lustre shimmer spray

disposable piping/pastry bag fitted with a 1-cm/½-in. round nozzle/tip

necklace template (see page 140)

transparent silicone mat

small disposable piping/pastry bag for icing

MAKES 2

Preheat the oven to 160°C (325°F) Gas 3.

Prepare the Basic Macarons according to the recipe on page 11, but add the honey gold food colouring paste before folding the egg whites into the dry ingredients. Put the mixture into a piping/pastry bag fitted with a 1-cm/½-in. round nozzle/tip.

Place the Necklace template on a baking sheet, and place a transparent silicone mat on top. Pipe the mixture onto the silicone mat, using the template as a guide.

Tap the bottom of the sheet lightly on the work surface to settle the mixture. Carefully slide the template out from under the silicone mat. Repeat to make two necklaces. Leave the macarons to rest for 15–30 minutes.

Bake the macarons on the middle shelf of the preheated oven for 15 minutes, until the tops are crisp and the undersides of the macarons are dry. Leave to cool for 30 minutes on the baking tray.

To decorate
Spray the shells with the edible pearl lustre. Use the Royal Icing to attach the sugar diamonds to the larger rounds of the necklace, as shown in the picture opposite, and the pearls around the diamonds. Reserve a pearl for each of the smaller rounds.

Leave to dry for 1 hour before moving the necklaces.

Variation
If you like, you can add a Buttercream filling (see page 24) and sandwich the two necklaces together.

celebrations

Chinese New Year is a great opportunity for a classy feast of colour in the form of these macaron lanterns. If you want to hang these for decoration, and not for eating, thread some wire through the filling.

Chinese New Year

FOR THE MACARON SHELLS

1 batch Basic Macarons (see recipe, page 11)

5 g/1 teaspoon extra red food colouring paste

FOR THE FILLING

2–3 tablespoons mandarin orange conserve

1 batch Chocolate Ganache (see recipe, page 23)

TO DECORATE

2.5 g/½ teaspoon primrose yellow food colouring paste

30 g/1 oz. white sugarpaste/fondant

gold food colouring powder

rejuvenating spirit to dilute the colouring powder

disposable piping/pastry bag fitted with a 1-cm/½-in. round nozzle/tip

5.5-cm/2¼-in. round template (see page 138)

transparent silicone mat

4.5-cm/1¾-in. round template (see page 138)

3.5-cm/1⅜-in. round template (see page 138)

2.5-cm/1-in. round template (see page 138)

small slim paintbrush

MAKES 40

Preheat the oven to 160°C (325°F) Gas 3.

Prepare the Basic Macarons according to the recipe on page 11, but add the extra red food colouring paste before folding the egg whites into the dry ingredients. Put the mixture into a piping/pastry bag fitted with a 1-cm/½-in. round nozzle/tip.

Place the 5.5-cm/2¼-in. round template on a baking sheet, and place a transparent silicone mat on top. Pipe 20 rounds onto the silicone mat, using the template as a guide. Repeat the steps above with the other 3 sizes. (You will need more than one baking sheet.) Tap the bottom of the sheets lightly on the work surface to settle the mixture. Carefully slide the template out from under the silicone mat. Leave the macarons to rest for 15–30 minutes.

Bake the macarons, one sheet at a time, on the middle shelf of the preheated oven: bake the 5.5-cm/2¼-in. macarons for 8 minutes, the 4.5-cm/1¾-in. macarons for 7 minutes, the 3.5-cm/1⅜-in. macarons for 6 minutes, and the 2.5-cm/1-in. macarons for 4 minutes, until the tops are crisp and the undersides of the macarons are dry. Leave to cool for 30 minutes on the baking sheets.

To make the filling, mix the mandarin orange conserve into the Chocolate Ganache.

Spread a teaspoonful of the filling mixture onto the flat-side of half of the macarons, and top with a macaron of matching size, pressing them together gently. Leave to set in the refrigerator for at least 12 hours before serving.

To decorate

Add the yellow food colouring paste to the white sugarpaste/fondant. Knead until the colour is even, then roll out to a thickness of 3 mm/⅛ in. Shape into half-moons in four different sizes to make the tops and bottoms of the lanterns.

While it is still soft, stick the sugarpaste/fondant to the tops and bottoms of the macarons before it dries.

Add a little rejuvenating spirit to the gold food colouring powder to dilute it. Use the paintbrush to paint the lines of the Chinese Lanterns. Leave to dry for 1 hour.

Children of all ages will delight in their very own flock of characterful Easter chicks. There's no need to limit them to Easter – they would make a welcome addition to party fare at any time of the year.

Easter chicks

FOR THE MACARON SHELLS
1 batch Basic Macarons
(see recipe, page 11)

3 g/⅔ teaspoon melon food colouring paste

TO DECORATE
1 batch Royal Icing (see recipe, page 29)

black food colouring paste

orange food colouring paste

disposable piping/pastry bag fitted with a 1-cm/½-in. round nozzle/tip

Easter Chicks template (see page 139)

transparent silicone mat

2 small disposable piping/pastry bags for icing

MAKES 60

Preheat the oven to 160°C (325°F) Gas 3.

Prepare the Basic Macarons according to the recipe on page 11, but add the melon food colouring paste before folding the egg whites into the dry ingredients. Put the mixture into a piping/pastry bag fitted with a 1-cm/½-in. round nozzle/tip.

Place the chicks template on a baking sheet, and place a transparent silicone mat on top. Pipe 60 chicks, using the template as a guide: start with a round head, then pipe a slightly larger round body, and drag the tail with a flick. (You will need more than one baking sheet.)

Tap the bottom of the sheet lightly on the work surface to settle the mixture. Carefully slide the template out from under the silicone mat. Leave the macarons to rest for 15–30 minutes.

Bake the macarons, one sheet at a time, on the middle shelf of the preheated oven for 8 minutes, until the tops are crisp and the undersides of the macarons are dry. Leave to cool for 30 minutes on the baking sheet.

To decorate

Make the Royal Icing recipe and, using a cocktail stick/toothpick, add enough black food colouring paste to create a dark shade for the eyes to about a third of the mixture. Transfer to one of the small piping/pastry bags. Snip off the end to create a small hole and pipe an eye onto each chick.

In the same way, add the orange food colouring paste to the remaining Royal Icing, transfer to the other piping bag and pipe on the beaks and feathers. Leave to dry for 1 hour.

Make a batch of these deliciously spine-chilling spiders for a Halloween
party and watch your guests try to decide whether to scream and run,
or brave it out and gobble one up!

spiders

FOR THE MACARON SHELLS
1 batch Basic Macarons
(see recipe, page 11)

5 g/1 teaspoon extra black food
colouring paste

FOR THE FILLING
100 g/3½ oz. marshmallow fluff

TO DECORATE
30 g/1 oz. white
sugarpaste/fondant

black food colouring paste

1 batch Royal Icing (see recipe,
page 29)

*disposable piping/pastry bag fitted
with a 1-cm/½-in. round nozzle/tip*

*5-cm/2-in. round template
(see page 138)*

transparent silicone mat

*2 small disposable piping/pastry
bags for icing*

MAKES 40

Preheat the oven to 160°C (325°F) Gas 3.

Prepare the Basic Macarons according to the recipe on page 11, but add the
extra black food colouring paste before folding the egg whites into the dry
ingredients. Put the mixture into a piping/pastry bag fitted with a 1-cm/½-in.
round nozzle/tip.

Place the 5-cm/2 in. round template on a baking sheet, and place a transparent
silicone mat on top. Pipe 80 macarons, using the template as a guide. (You will
need more than one baking sheet.) Tap the bottom of the sheets lightly on the
work surface to settle the mixture. Carefully slide the template out from under the
silicone mat. Leave the macarons to rest for 15–30 minutes.

Bake the macarons, one sheet at a time, on the middle shelf of the preheated
oven for 8 minutes, until the tops are crisp and the undersides of the macarons
are dry. Leave to cool for 30 minutes on the baking sheet.

Make the marshmallow fluff for the filling by following the packet instructions.

Using a teaspoon, place a little filling mixture onto half of the shells, and
sandwich the pairs together gently to create 40 macaron spider bodies. Decorate
and serve immediately.

To decorate
Use a cocktail stick/toothpick to add some black food colouring paste to the white
sugarpaste/fondant. Knead until the colour is even. Make the legs by rolling the
paste out into long thin sausages. Cut the lengths to make 8 for each spider. Use
the filling to attach the legs in between the macaron shells.

Next, make the Royal Icing and divide it into two portions. Transfer one portion to
a small piping/pastry bag and snip off the end to create a small hole. Pipe 8 white
eyes on the top of each spider.

Use a cocktail stick/toothpick to add enough black food colouring paste to the
other portion to create a dark shade. Transfer to the other small piping/pastry bag
and snip off the end to create a small hole. Pipe eyeballs on the top of each white
eye. Leave to dry for 1 hour.

BOO! Make these spooky ghosts to glide among the fearsome spiders found on page 108. They are fantastic little phantoms, guaranteed to make any Halloween party go with a swoon.

ghosts

FOR THE MACARON SHELLS
1 batch Basic Macarons
(see recipe, page 11)

TO DECORATE
30 g/1 oz. white
sugarpaste/fondant

1 batch Royal Icing (see recipe,
page 29)

black food colouring paste

*disposable piping/pastry bag fitted
with a 1-cm/½-in. round nozzle/tip*

Ghost Template (see page 139)

transparent silicone mat

*small disposable piping/pastry bag
for icing*

MAKES 80

Preheat the oven to 160°C (325°F) Gas 3.

Prepare the Basic Macarons according to the recipe on page 11. No food colouring is added. Put the mixture into a piping/pastry bag fitted with a 1-cm/½-in. round nozzle/tip.

Place the Ghost template on a baking sheet, and place a transparent silicone mat on top. Pipe 80 macarons, using the template as a guide. Start each one at the top of the head and finish by dragging the tail with a flick. (You will need more than one baking sheet.) Tap the bottom of the sheets lightly on the work surface to settle the mixture. Carefully slide the template out from under the silicone mat. Leave the macarons to rest for 15–30 minutes.

Bake the macarons, one sheet at a time, on the middle shelf of the preheated oven for 8 minutes, until the tops are crisp and the undersides of the macarons are dry. Leave to cool for 30 minutes on the baking sheet.

To decorate

Place the ghost template underneath the silicone mat again. Knead the white sugarpaste/fondant until it is evenly mixed, then roll it out on the mat to a thickness of 3 mm/⅛ in and use a knife to cut out ghost shapes. While it is still soft, mould the sugarpaste/fondant ghosts over the macaron biscuits. You may need to do this in batches. Leave to dry.

Next, make the Royal Icing and use a cocktail stick/toothpick to add enough black food colouring paste to create a dark shade. Transfer to the small piping/pastry bag and snip off the end to create a small hole. Pipe eyes and hoo-ing mouths on each ghost. Leave to dry for 1 hour.

Whether you are welcoming in the New Year, celebrating the 4th of July, or having a bonfire party, fireworks help the event go with a bang. These edible versions have a paprika-kick of their own.

fireworks

FOR THE MACARON SHELLS
2 batches Basic Macarons
(see recipe, page 11)

5 g/1 teaspoon extra black food colouring paste

FOR THE FILLING
hot paprika, to taste

1 batch Chocolate Ganache
(see recipe, page 23)

TO DECORATE
1 batch Royal Icing (see recipe, page 29)

5 g/1 teaspoon yellow food colouring paste

5 g/1 teaspoon Egyptian orange food colouring paste

5 g/1 teaspoon fuchsia pink food colouring paste

5 g/1 teaspoon royal blue food colouring paste

disposable piping/pastry bag fitted with a 1-cm/½-in. round nozzle/tip

*5-cm/2-in. round template
(see page 138)*

transparent silicone mat

4 small disposable piping/pastry bags for icing

MAKES 40

Preheat the oven to 160°C (325°F) Gas 3.

Prepare the first batch of Basic Macarons according to the recipe on page 11, but add the extra black food colouring paste before folding the egg whites into the dry ingredients. Put the mixture into a piping/pastry bag fitted with a 1-cm/½-in. round nozzle/tip.

Place the 5-cm/2 in. round template on a baking sheet, and place a transparent silicone mat on top. Pipe 80 macarons, using the template as a guide. (You will need more than one baking sheet.) Tap the bottom of the sheets lightly on the work surface to settle the mixture. Carefully slide the template out from under the silicone mat. Leave the macarons to rest for 15–30 minutes.

Bake the macarons, one sheet at a time, on the middle shelf of the preheated oven for 8 minutes, until the tops are crisp and the undersides of the macarons are dry. Leave to cool for 30 minutes on the baking sheet.

For the filling, mix paprika into the Chocolate Ganache to taste.

Using a teaspoon, place a little of the chocolate filling mixture onto half of the shells, and sandwich the pairs together gently. Leave to set in the refrigerator for at least 12 hours before serving.

To decorate
Divide the Royal Icing into four portions. Add each of the food colouring pastes to one of the portions and mix until the colour is even. Transfer each to a small piping/pastry bag and snip off the ends to create small holes. Draw lines of firework sparklers on each of the macarons. Leave to dry for 1 hour.

Decorations known as runouts dress these trees. They are made by pouring runny Royal Icing onto parchment or acetate paper according to a shape beneath the paper. It takes 4 days to decorate and dry them properly, so make them well ahead.

Christmas tree

(see page 141)

FOR THE MACARON SHELLS
1 batch Basic Macarons
(see recipe, page 11)

5 g/1 teaspoon holly green food colouring paste

FOR THE FILLING
2–3 tablespoons cranberry preserve

1 batch Chocolate Ganache
(see recipe, page 23)

TO DECORATE
1 batch Royal Icing (see recipe, page 29)

assorted food colouring pastes

disposable piping/pastry bag fitted with a 1-cm/½-in. round nozzle/tip

*Christmas Tree template
(see page 141)*

transparent silicone mat

small disposable piping/pastry bags for icing (for the decoration)

small Christmas decorative templates, such as stockings, presents

6 sheets of A4 parchment paper or acetate paper

MAKES 5

Preheat the oven to 160°C (325°F) Gas 3.

Prepare the Basic Macarons according to the recipe on page 11, but add the holly green food colouring paste before folding the egg whites into the dry ingredients. Put the mixture into a piping/pastry bag fitted with a 1-cm/½-in. round nozzle/tip.

Place the tree template on a baking sheet, and place a transparent silicone mat on top. Using the template as a guide, pipe 10 trees, leaving a tiny gap between the circles in each tree to allow for expansion during baking. (You will need more than one baking sheet.) Tap the bottom of the sheets lightly on the work surface to settle the mixture. Carefully slide the template out from under the silicone mat. Leave the macarons to rest for 35–40 minutes.

Bake the macarons, one sheet at a time, on the middle shelf of the preheated oven for 15 minutes, until the tops are crisp and the undersides of the macarons are dry. Leave to cool for 30 minutes on the baking sheet.

To make the filling, mix the cranberry preserve into the Chocolate Ganache.

Spread some filling onto the flat-side of one tree shell and sandwich together with another. Repeat with the remaining macaron shells to make 5 trees. Handle the trees very gently. Leave to set in the refrigerator for at least 12 hours before serving.

To decorate
Make the Royal Icing and divide it into as many portions as you have colours, plus one to leave white. Fill one of the small piping bags with the white portion. Place the stocking templates underneath the paper. Outline the shapes with the Royal Icing, then fill them in. Repeat using the present templates and the coloured icing. It is wise to make plenty of extra decorations as runouts are delicate. Leave them to dry for 48 hours before decorating the top.

Make a new batch of Royal Icing, and decorate the plain stockings and presents with coloured icing strips. Leave to dry for a further 48 hours. Use fresh icing to stick the dried runouts on the macaron Christmas trees.

Although these jolly snowmen will be a hit at Christmas, they need not be confined to the festive season. Make them when the weather is cold, or for a winter-themed party at any time of year.

snowmen

FOR THE MACARON SHELLS
1 batch Basic Macarons
(see recipe, page 11)

FOR THE FILLING
50 g/2 oz. candied chestnuts,
finely chopped
1 batch Buttercream (see recipe,
page 23)

FOR THE DECORATION
1 batch Royal Icing (see recipe,
page 29)
black food colouring paste
tangerine food colouring paste
holly green food colouring paste
royal blue food colouring paste
Christmas red food colouring
paste
icing/confectioners' sugar, for
dusting

*disposable piping/pastry bag fitted
with a 1-cm/½-in. round nozzle/tip*
Snowman template (see page 139)
transparent silicone mat
*5 small disposable piping/pastry bags
for icing (for the decoration)*

MAKES 25

Preheat the oven to 160°C (325°F) Gas 3.

Prepare the Basic Macarons according to the recipe on page 11. Put the mixture into the piping/pastry bag fitted with a 1-cm/½-in. round nozzle/tip.

Place the Snowman template on a baking sheet, and place a transparent silicone mat on top. Using the template as a guide, pipe a snowman on to the silicone mat. Start at the top of the head then follow with the body. Repeat to make 25 snowmen (you will need more than one baking sheet).

Tap the bottom of the sheets lightly on the work surface to settle the mixture. Carefully slide the template out from under the silicone mat. Leave the macarons to rest for 20–40 minutes.

Bake the macarons, one sheet at a time, on the middle shelf of the preheated oven for 12 minutes, until the tops are crisp and the undersides of the macarons are dry. Leave to cool for 30 minutes on the baking sheets.

For the filling, mix the candied chestnuts into the Buttercream. Line the snowmen macarons into rows of 2, flat-side up. Using a teaspoon, place a little chestnut filling mixture onto half of the shells, and sandwich the pairs together gently to create 25 macarons. Leave to set in the refrigerator for at least 12 hours before serving.

To decorate
Prepare the Royal Icing recipe, then divide it equally into 5 portions. Use a cocktail stick/toothpick to add a little of each food colouring paste to each portion and mix. Transfer the black to a small piping/pastry bag for icing, and snip off the end to create a small hole.

Pipe the eyes and buttons in black, then repeat with the tangerine in a second piping/pastry bag and give the snowmen carrot noses. Use the remaining three colours for the snowmen's scarves. Leave to dry for 1 hour, then lightly dust the macarons with icing/confectioners' sugar before serving.

These edible baubles will enhance the Christmas table (lay them flat; they're a little fragile to hang on the tree), or make a perfect gift. Make sure the cookie-cutter shapes fit on the macarons, and be creative with the Royal Icing.

Christmas baubles

FOR THE MACARON SHELLS

4 batches Basic Macarons
(see recipe, page 11)

4 g/¾ teaspoon lavender food
colouring paste

3 g/⅔ teaspoon daffodil food
colouring paste

5 g/1 teaspoon Egyptian orange
food colouring paste

5 g/1 teaspoon rose food
colouring paste

FOR THE FILLINGS

1 batch Chocolate Ganache
(see recipe, page 23)

200 g/7 oz chestnuts in syrup

60 g/2 oz honeycomb, crushed

1 batch Buttercream (see
recipe, page 24)

200 g/⅔ cup cranberry conserve

350 g/1¼ cups lemon curd

TO DECORATE

1 batch Royal Icing (see recipe,
page 29)

5 different food colouring pastes
(Christmas colours)

sugarpaste/fondant in assorted
colours

*4.5-cm/1¾-in. round template (see
page 138)*

transparent silicone mat

*4 disposable piping/pastry bags fitted
with 6-mm/¼-in. round nozzles/tips*

*5 small disposable piping/pastry bags
for icing*

assorted small Christmas cutters

MAKES 160

Preheat the oven to 160°C (325°F) Gas 3.

Prepare the first batch of Basic Macarons according to the recipe on page 11, but add the lavender food colouring paste before folding the egg whites into the dry ingredients. Put the mixture into a piping/pastry bag fitted with a 6-mm/¼-in. round nozzle/tip.

Place the 4.5-cm/1¾-in. round template on a baking sheet, and place a transparent silicone mat on top. Pipe 80 rounds onto the silicone mat, using the template as a guide. (You will need more than one baking sheet.) Tap the bottom of the sheets lightly on the work surface to settle the mixture. Carefully slide the template out from under the silicone mat. Leave the macarons to rest for 15–30 minutes.

Bake the macarons, one sheet at a time, on the middle shelf of the preheated oven for 8 minutes, until the tops are crisp and the undersides are dry. Leave the oven on and allow to cool for 30 minutes on the baking sheets.

Meanwhile, prepare and bake the remaining 3 batches of Basic Macarons in the same way, using the daffodil, Egyptian orange and rose food colouring pastes for each separate batch.

To make the fillings, finely chop the chestnuts and mix them into half of the Chocolate Ganache; mix the other half with the crushed honeycomb. Make the Buttercream filling, then fold the cranberry conserve into the Buttercream.

Line the coloured macarons into rows of 2, flat-side up. Using a teaspoon, place a little of the chocolate/chestnut filling mixture onto half of the purple shells, and sandwich the pairs together gently. Repeat for the other colours, using the chocolate honeycomb to fill the orange shells, the cranberry Buttercream for the pink shells and the lemon curd for the yellow shells. Leave to set in the refrigerator for at least 12 hours before serving.

To decorate

Make the Royal Icing recipe and keep a little aside to use to stick the sugarpaste/fondant decorations on (see below). Divide the rest into 5 portions and use cocktail sticks/toothpicks to mix in the food colouring pastes. Transfer each to a small piping/pastry bag for icing, and snip off the end to create a small hole. Set aside 20 macarons, then use the coloured icings to pipe Christmas patterns on the remaining baubles.

Roll out the sugarpaste/fondant to a thickness of 3 mm/⅛ in. and use the cookie cutters to stamp out 20 tiny Christmas shapes. Use the reserved Royal Icing to stick them onto the reserved macaron shells. Leave to dry for 1 hour.

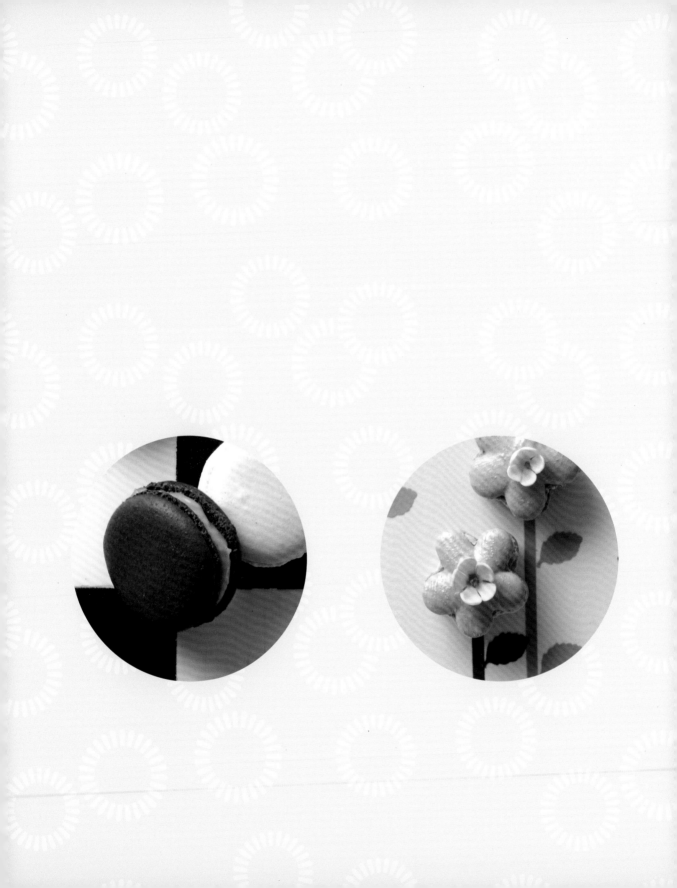

game, set & match

Straightforward ingredients, such as popping candy, are ideal for kids. With a good selection of coloured squares and circles they will have as much fun creating their own designs as they would with Lego blocks.

building block cars

FOR THE MACARON SHELLS

6 batches Basic Macarons (see recipe, page 11) – 1 batch for each colour

4 g/¾ teaspoon gooseberry food colouring paste

3 g/⅔ teaspoon dark brown food colouring paste

0.5 g/scant ⅛ teaspoon red colouring paste

5 g/1 teaspoon extra black food colouring paste

5 g/1 teaspoon extra red food colouring paste

4 g/¾ teaspoon egg yellow food colouring paste

3 g/⅔ teaspoon mint green food colouring paste

FOR THE FILLING

1 batch Chocolate Ganache (see recipe, page 23)

1 batch Caramel Chocolate Ganache (see recipe, page 24)

20 g/¾ oz popping candy

6 disposable piping/pastry bags fitted with 6-mm/¼-in. nozzles/tips

3-cm/1¼-in. square template (see page 139)

2.5-cm/1-in. round template (see page 138)

transparent silicone mat

MAKES ABOUT 15 CARS

Preheat the oven to 160°C (325°F) Gas 3.

Prepare the first batch of Basic Macarons according to the recipe on page 11, but add the gooseberry food colouring paste before folding the egg whites into the dry ingredients. Put the mixture into a piping/pastry bag fitted with a 6-mm/¼-in. round nozzle/tip.

Place the square template on a baking sheet, and place a transparent silicone mat on top. Pipe the mixture onto the silicone mat, using the template as a guide, filling each square carefully. Carry on until the mixture is used up. (You may need more than one baking sheet.)

Tap the bottom of the sheet lightly on the work surface to settle the mixture. Carefully slide the template out from under the silicone mat. Leave the macarons to rest for 15–30 minutes.

Repeat for the brown square blocks, adding the dark brown and red food colouring paste before folding the egg whites into the dry ingredients.

For the wheels, prepare the Basic Macarons according to the recipe on page 11, but add the extra black food colouring paste before folding the egg whites into the dry ingredients. Put the mixture into a piping/pastry bag fitted with a 6-mm/¼-in. round nozzle/tip.

Place the round template on a baking sheet, and place a transparent silicone mat on top. Pipe round macarons onto the silicone mat, using the template as a guide. (You may need more than one baking sheet.)

Tap the bottom of the sheet lightly on the work surface as before, carefully slide the template out from under the silicone mat and leave the macarons to rest for 15–30 minutes.

Repeat with a further 3 batches for the traffic lights, using the extra red, egg yellow and mint green food colouring pastes.

Bake the macarons, one sheet at a time, on the middle shelf of the preheated oven for 6 minutes, until the tops are crisp and the undersides of the macarons are dry. Leave to cool for 30 minutes on the baking sheet.

Place the macaron shells in two rows. Spread some Chocolate Ganache or Caramel Chocolate Ganache onto the flat-sides of half the shells, sprinkle with popping candy and top with the remaining shells, pressing them together gently.

Assemble into cars and traffic lights, or allow the children to do so – one suggestion is in the picture opposite. You will have plenty of building blocks, which will make varying cars depending on how you assemble them.

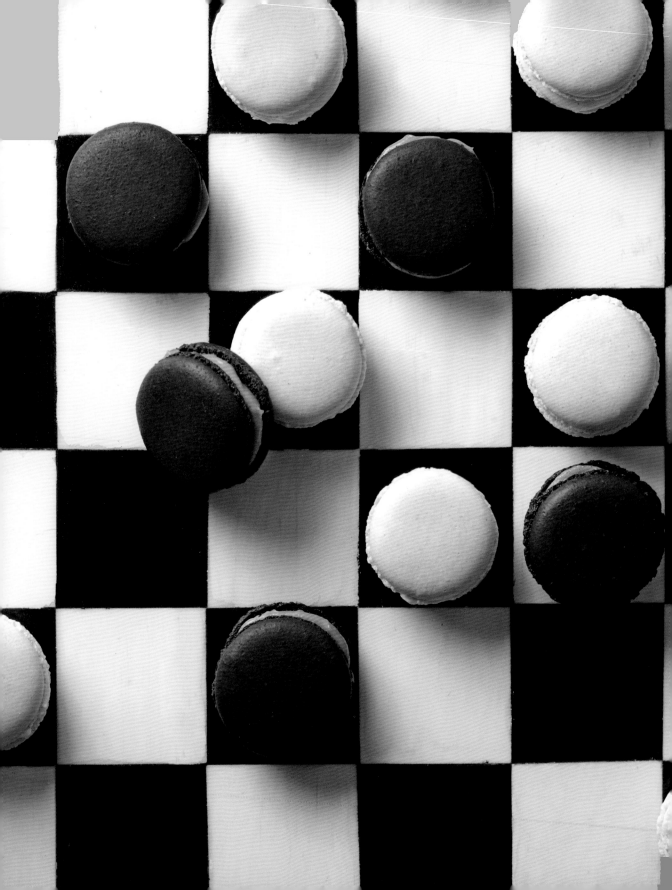

A game of draughts or checkers will never be the same again – in this version you get to eat each piece you take! The passionfruit adds an extra zing to the Caramel Chocolate Ganche filling.

draughts

FOR THE MACARON SHELLS

2 batches Basic Macarons (see recipe, page 11)

5 g/1 teaspoon extra black food colouring paste

5 g/1 teaspoon superwhite icing whitener colouring powder

FOR THE FILLING

1 batch Caramel Chocolate Ganache (see recipe, page 24)

20 g/¾ oz dried passionfruit, chopped

1 batch Buttercream (see recipe, page 24)

20 fresh raspberries

2 disposable piping/pastry bags fitted with 1-cm/½-in. round nozzles/tips

5-cm/2-in. round template (see page 138)

transparent silicone mat

MAKES 40

Preheat the oven to 160°C (325°F) Gas 3.

Prepare the first batch of Basic Macarons according to the recipe on page 11, but add the extra black food colouring paste before folding the egg whites into the dry ingredients. Put the mixture into a piping/pastry bag fitted with a 1-cm/½-in. round nozzle/tip.

Place the 5-cm/2-in. round template on a baking sheet, and place a transparent silicone mat on top. Pipe 40 macarons onto the silicone mat, using the template as a guide. (You may need more than one baking sheet.)

Tap the bottom of the sheet lightly on the work surface to settle the mixture. Carefully slide the template out from under the silicone mat. Leave the macarons to rest for 15–30 minutes.

Bake the macarons, one sheet at a time, on the middle shelf of the preheated oven for 8 minutes, until the tops are crisp and the undersides of the macarons are dry. Leave to cool for 30 minutes on the baking sheet. Leave the oven on.

Meanwhile, prepare the second batch of Basic Macarons according to the recipe on page 11, but add the superwhite food colouring powder before folding the egg whites into the dry ingredients. Then continue as above.

Add the chopped passionfruit to the Caramel Chocolate Ganache. Place the black shells in two rows. Spread the filling onto the flat-sides of half the shells and top with the remaining shells, pressing them together gently.

Place the white shells in two rows and spread the flat-sides of half the shells with Buttercream. Put a raspberry in the centre of each one and cover with another drop of Buttercream. Top with the remaining shells, pressing them together gently.

Chill the macarons for 2 hours before serving.

Smacs are my macaron invention – perfect for sharing with friends. They are so pretty and colourful, these joined rows of macarons will enhance any teatime.

Smacs

For the macaron shells

4 batches Basic Macarons (see recipe, page 11)

4 g/¾ teaspoon gooseberry food colouring paste

3 g/⅔ teaspoon daffodil yellow food colouring paste

5 g/1 teaspoon Egyptian orange food colouring paste

5 g/1 teaspoon rose food colouring paste

about 150 chocolate chips

For the filling

30 g/2 tablespoons sesame seeds, plus extra for sprinkling

1 batch Caramel Chocolate Ganache (see recipe, page 24)

1 batch Chocolate Ganache (see recipe, page 23)

1 batch Buttercream (see recipe, page 24)

20 g/¾ oz. dried red berries, chopped, plus extra for sprinkling

4 disposable piping/pastry bags fitted with 6-mm/¼-in. nozzles/tips

Smac template (see page 141)

transparent silicone mat

Makes 30 of each colour

Preheat the oven to 160°C (325°F) Gas 3.

Prepare the first batch of Basic Macarons according to the recipe on page 11, but add the gooseberry food colouring paste before before folding the egg whites into the dry ingredients. Put the mixture into a piping/pastry bag fitted with a 6-mm/¼-in. round nozzle/tip.

Place the Smac template on a baking sheet, and place a transparent silicone mat on top. Pipe the macaron mixture onto the silicone mat, using the template as a guide. Leave a tiny space between each circle to allow for expansion. (You may need more than one baking sheet.)

Tap the bottom of the sheet lightly on the work surface to settle the mixture. Carefully slide the template out from under the silicone mat. Leave the macarons to rest for 15–30 minutes.

Repeat the above, using the daffodil yellow, Egyptian orange and rose food colouring pastes.

Sprinkle sesame seeds onto the green row and dried red berries onto the pink row before putting them into the oven. Decorate the orange smacs with chocolate chips.

Bake the macarons, one sheet at a time, on the middle shelf of the preheated oven for 10 minutes, until the tops are crisp and the undersides of the macarons are dry. Leave to cool for 30 minutes on the baking sheet.

For the fillings, lightly fry the sesame seeds in a pan and then grind into a paste using a mortar and pestle. Add the sesame paste to the Caramel Chocolate Ganache. Place the green macaron shells in two rows. Spread the chocolate sesame mixture onto the flat-sides of half the shells and top with the remaining shells, pressing them together gently.

Fill the yellow and orange shells with Chocolate Ganache.

Mix the chopped dried berries into the Buttercream, then fill the pink shells with this mixture.

Leave to set in the refrigerator for at least 12 hours before serving.

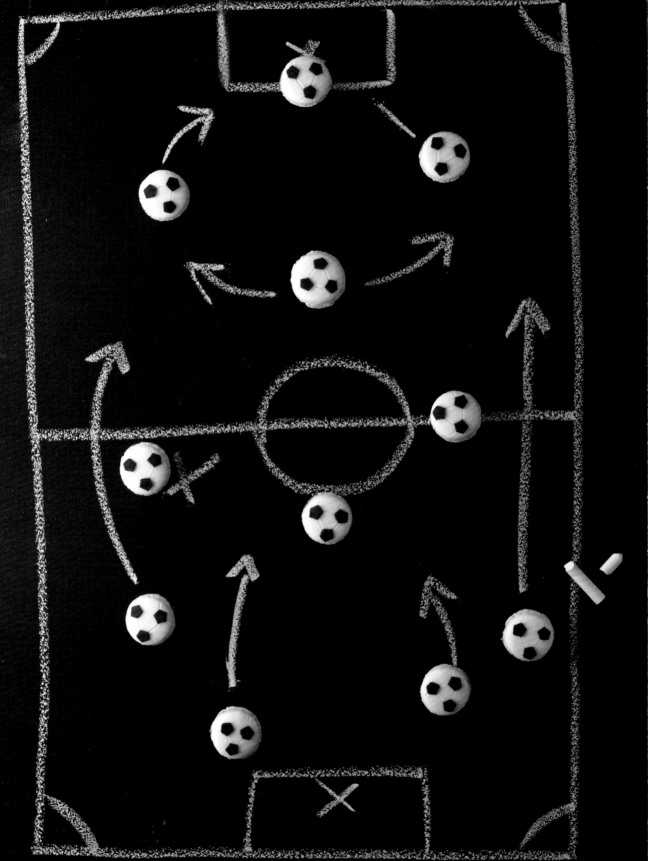

Little macarons that will be instantly familiar – fans of one of the world's most popular games will be entranced. These sporty biscuits mean that soccer will be re-enacted on your tabletop.

footballs

FOR THE MACARON SHELLS
1 batch Basic Macarons (see recipe, page 11)

FOR THE FILLING
200 g/ scant 1 cup chocolate hazelnut spread

TO DECORATE
30 g/1 oz. white sugarpaste/fondant

10 g/⅓ oz. black sugarpaste/fondant

disposable piping/pastry bag fitted with a 1-cm/½-in. round nozzle/tip

4-cm/1½-in. round template (see page 138)

transparent silicone mat

disposable piping/pastry bag fitted with a 2-mm/¹∕₁₆-in. round nozzle/tip

5-cm/2-in. round cutter

bamboo stick

MAKES 40

Preheat the oven to 160°C (325°F) Gas 3.

Prepare the Basic Macarons according to the recipe on page 11. No food colouring is added. Put the mixture into a piping/pastry bag fitted with a 1-cm/½-in. round nozzle/tip.

Place the 4-cm/1½-in. round template on a baking sheet, and place a transparent silicone mat on top. Pipe 80 round macarons onto the silicone mat, using the template as a guide. (You may need more than one baking sheet.)

Tap the bottom of the sheet lightly on the work surface to settle the mixture. Carefully slide the template out from under the silicone mat. Leave the macarons to rest for 15–30 minutes.

Bake the macarons, one sheet at a time, on the middle shelf of the preheated oven for 8 minutes, until the tops are crisp and the undersides of the macarons are dry. Leave to cool for 30 minutes on the baking sheet.

Place the macaron shells in two rows. Spread the chocolate hazelnut spread onto the flat-sides of half the shells and top with the remaining shells, pressing them together gently. Leave to set in the refrigerator for at least 12 hours before serving.

To decorate
Knead the white sugarpaste/fondant until evenly mixed. Roll out the paste onto a transparent silicone mat and cut circles with the 5-cm/2-in. round cutter. While it is soft, mould the sugarpaste/fondant over each macaron. Use a bamboo stick to draw lines in it in a typical football/soccer ball pattern.

Knead the black sugarpaste, roll thinly and cut small polygons to resemble the black patches on a football/soccer ball. Stick the black patches onto the white sugarpaste/fondant with a little water. Leave to dry for 1 hour.

These easy-to-make treats, filled with a version of strawberries and cream,
are ideal fare whenever the major tennis tournaments are hitting the headlines.

tennis balls

FOR THE MACARON SHELLS
1 batch Basic Macarons
(see recipe, page 11)

3 g/⅔ teaspoon gooseberry food
colouring paste

1 g/¼ teaspoon lime green food
colouring paste

FOR THE FILLING
1 batch Buttercream (see recipe,
page 24)

fresh strawberries

TO DECORATE
1 batch Royal Icing (see recipe,
page 29)

*disposable piping/pastry bag fitted
with a 1-cm/½-in. round nozzle/tip*

*5-cm/2-in. round template
(see page 138)*

transparent silicone mat

*small disposable piping/pastry bag
for icing*

MAKES 40

Preheat the oven to 160°C (325°F) Gas 3.

Prepare the Basic Macarons according to the recipe on page 11, but add the
gooseberry and lime green food colouring pastes before folding the egg whites
into the dry ingredients. Put the mixture into a piping/pastry bag fitted with a
1-cm/½-in. round nozzle/tip.

Place the 5-cm/2-in. round template on a baking sheet, and place a transparent
silicone mat on top. Pipe 80 round macarons onto the silicone mat, using the
template as a guide. (You may need more than one baking sheet.)

Tap the bottom of the sheet lightly on the work surface to settle the mixture.
Carefully slide the template out from under the silicone mat. Leave the macarons
to rest for 15–30 minutes.

Bake the macarons, one sheet at a time, on the middle shelf of the preheated
oven for 8 minutes, until the tops are crisp and the undersides of the macarons
are dry. Leave to cool for 30 minutes on the baking sheet.

Make the Buttercream filling, chop the strawberries and lightly fold them into the
Buttercream. Carefully spread the mixture onto the flat-sides of half the shells
and top with the remaining shells, pressing them together gently. Chill in the
refrigerator for 2 hours before serving.

To decorate
Prepare the Royal Icing according to the recipe on page 29. Using the small
piping/pastry bag for icing, pipe the lines as seen on tennis balls. Leave to dry
for 1 hour.

No need to wait until the Rugby World Cup, the Six Nations Championship or even the Aussie Rules International Cup, to make these chocolate- and caramel-filled rugby balls. Enthusiasts of all ages will enjoy them anytime!

rugby balls

FOR THE MACARON SHELLS
1 batch Basic Macarons
(see recipe, page 11)

4 g/¾ teaspoon dark brown food colouring paste

FOR THE FILLING
1 batch Chocolate Ganache
(see recipe, page 23)

1 batch Caramel Chocolate Ganache (see recipe, page 24)

1 Batch Buttercream (see recipe, page 24)

FOR THE DECORATION
1 batch Royal Icing (see recipe, page 29)

black food colouring paste

disposable piping/pastry bag fitted with a 6-mm/¼-in. round nozzle/tip

Rugby Ball template (see page 139)

transparent silicone mat

small disposable piping/pastry bag for icing (for the decoration)

MAKES 30

Preheat the oven to 160°C (325°F) Gas 3.

Prepare the Basic Macarons according to the recipe on page 11, but add the dark brown food colouring paste before before folding the egg whites into the dry ingredients. Put the mixture into a piping/pastry bag fitted with a 6-mm/¼-in. round nozzle/tip.

Place the Rugby Ball template on a baking sheet, and place a transparent silicone mat on top. Pipe the outline of the Rugby Ball onto the silicone mat, using the template as a guide. Fill in carefully wth the macaron mixture and repeat to make 60 ball shapes. (You may need more than one baking sheet.)

Tap the bottom of the sheets lightly on the work surface to settle the mixture. Carefully slide the template out from under the silicone mat. Leave the macarons to rest for 15–30 minutes.

Bake the macarons, one sheet at a time, on the middle shelf of the preheated oven for 8 minutes, until the tops are crisp and the undersides of the macarons are dry. Leave to cool for 30 minutes on the baking sheet.

For the filling, spread the Caramel Chocolate Ganache onto the flat-sides of 10 macaron shells, spread the Chocolate Ganache onto the flat-sides of 10 macaron shells and spread the Buttercream onto the flat-sides of 10 macaron shells. Top with the remaining shells, pressing them together gently. Leave to set in the refrigerator for at least 12 hours before serving.

To decorate
Prepare the Royal Icing according to the recipe on page 29. Use a cocktail stick/toothpick to add a little of the black food colouring paste to the icing and mix well. Transfer to a small piping/pastry bag for icing, and snip off the end to create a small hole. Pipe the lacing lines as shown in the picture on each of the rugby balls. Leave to dry for 1 hour.

Celebrate Cool Britannia by making bunting out of these cheerful Union Jack macarons. If you are feeling truly international, why not recreate other national flags for a real United Nations effect instead?

flags

FOR THE MACARON SHELLS

1 batch Basic Macarons
(see recipe, page 11)

3 g/⅔ teaspoon lime green food colouring paste

1 g/¼ teaspoon mint green food colouring paste

FOR THE FILLING

1 batch Buttercream (see recipe, page 24)

3 tablespoons apple conserve

FOR THE DECORATION

5 g/1 teaspoon navy blue food colouring paste

5 g/1 teaspoon red food colouring paste

5 g/1 teaspoon pearl food colouring powder

rejuvenating spirit to dilute the colouring powder

disposable piping/pastry bag fitted with a 1-cm/½-in. round nozzle/tip

5-cm/2-in. round template (see page 138)

transparent silicone mat

flat paintbrush

2 slim pointed-tipped paintbrushes

MAKES 40

Preheat the oven to 160°C (325°F) Gas 3.

Prepare the Basic Macarons according to the recipe on page 11, but add the lime green and mint green food colouring pastes before folding the egg whites into the dry ingredients. Put the mixture into a piping/pastry bag fitted with a 1-cm/½-in. round nozzle/tip.

Place the 5-cm/2-in. round template on a baking sheet, and place a transparent silicone mat on top. Pipe 80 round macarons onto the silicone mat, using the template as a guide. (You may need more than one baking sheet.)

Tap the bottom of the sheet lightly on the work surface to settle the mixture. Carefully slide the template out from under the silicone mat. Leave the macarons to rest for 15–30 minutes.

Bake the macarons, one sheet at a time, on the middle shelf of the preheated oven for 8 minutes, until the tops are crisp and the undersides of the macarons are dry. Leave to cool for 30 minutes on the baking sheet.

Lightly fold the apple conserve into the Buttercream. Carefully spread the mixture onto the flat-sides of half the shells and top with the remaining shells, pressing them together gently. Leave to set in the refrigerator for at least 12 hours before serving.

To decorate

Add a little rejuvenating spirit to the navy blue, red and pearl food colourings to dilute them. Use the flat brush to paint the red lines of the Union Jack and one of the slim brushes to fill in the blue colours. Finish off with thin white outlines around the flag using the second pointed-tipped brush. Leave to dry for 1 hour.

Mary, Mary, quite contrary, how does your garden grow? There is absolutely
nothing contrary about these pretty maids all in a row.

felt flowers

FOR THE MACARON SHELLS

5 batches Basic Macarons
(see recipe, page 11)

3 g/⅔ teaspoon lavender food
colouring paste

3 g/⅔ teaspoon primrose food
colouring paste

5 g/1 teaspoon Egyptian orange
food colouring paste

5 g/1 teaspoon rose food
colouring paste

3.5 g/generous ⅔ teaspoon royal
blue food colouring paste

FOR THE FILLINGS

1 batch White Chocolate Ganache
(see recipe, page 23)

150 g/½ cup cassis conserve

150 g/½ cup lemon curd

2–3 drops rose essence oil

1 batch Buttercream (see recipe,
page 24)

150 g/½ cup gooseberry conserve

150 g/½ cup blueberry jam/jelly

FOR THE DECORATION

20 g/¾ oz. white sugarpaste/
fondant

1 batch Royal Icing (see recipe,
page 29)

2.5 g/½ teaspoon orange food
colouring paste

*5 disposable piping/pastry bags fitted
with 6-mm/¼-in. round nozzles/tips*

Flower template (see page 140)

transparent silicone mat

*small disposable piping/pastry bag
for icing*

tiny flower cutter

MAKES 35 FOR EACH COLOUR

Preheat the oven to 160°C (325°F) Gas 3.

Prepare the first Basic Macaron batch according to the recipe on page 11,
but add the lavender food colouring paste before folding the egg whites into the
dry ingredients. Put the mixture into a piping/pastry bag fitted with a 6-mm/¼-in.
round nozzle/tip.

Place the Flower template on a baking sheet, and place a transparent silicone
mat on top. Using the template as a guide, start piping from the outer edge of
the petals and gently pull inwards to fill in the flower. Repeat to make 70 flowers.
(You may need more than one baking sheet.) Tap the bottom of the sheets lightly
on the work surface to settle the mixture. Carefully slide the template out from
under the silicone mat. Leave the macarons to rest for 15–30 minutes.

Bake the macarons, one sheet at a time, on the middle shelf of the preheated
oven for 10 minutes, until the tops are crisp and the undersides of the macarons
are dry. Leave to cool for 30 minutes on the baking sheet.

Meanwhile, prepare and bake the remaining 4 batches of Basic Macarons in the
same way, using the yellow, orange, red and blue food colouring pastes for each
separate batch of flowers.

Divide the White Chocolate Ganache filling into three portions. Add the cassis
conserve to one portion of the White Chocolate Ganache and use this mixture to
fill the lavender flowers. Add the lemon curd to the second portion of
buttercream and use this mixture to fill the orange flowers. Add the rose essence
oil to the third portion of White Chocolate Ganache and use this mixture to fill the
rose flowers.

Divide the Buttercream into two portions. Add the gooseberry conserve to one
portion and use this mixture to fill the primrose flowers. Add the blueberry
jam/jelly to the second portion and use this mixture to fill the blue flowers. Make
sure that all the petals align. Leave to set in the refrigerator for at least 12 hours
before serving.

To decorate

Knead the white sugarpaste/fondant until softened. Roll out the
sugarpaste/fondant and use a tiny flower cutter to cut about 175 flowers.

Add the orange food colouring paste to the Royal Icing, mixing well. Fill the small
piping/pastry bag for icing and pipe tiny dots in the middle of the flowers. Use the
rest of the icing to stick the flowers onto the centre of the macarons. Leave to dry
for 1 hour.

templates

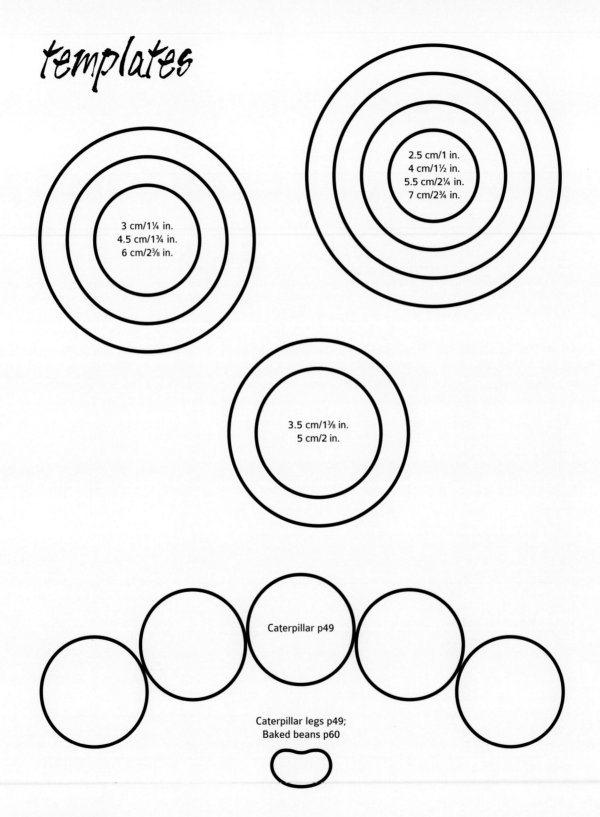

3 cm/1¼ in.
4.5 cm/1¾ in.
6 cm/2⅜ in.

2.5 cm/1 in.
4 cm/1½ in.
5.5 cm/2¼ in.
7 cm/2¾ in.

3.5 cm/1⅜ in.
5 cm/2 in.

Caterpillar p49

Caterpillar legs p49;
Baked beans p60

Heart p73

Chicks p107

Ghost p111

Rugby ball p133

Toast p60

3 cm/1¼ in. square

Snowman p116

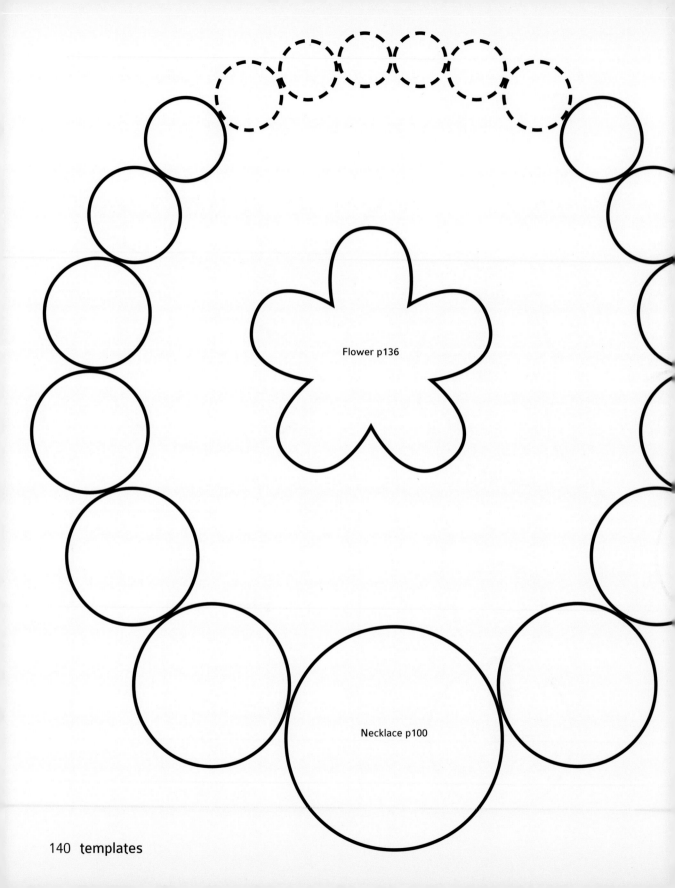

Flower p136

Necklace p100

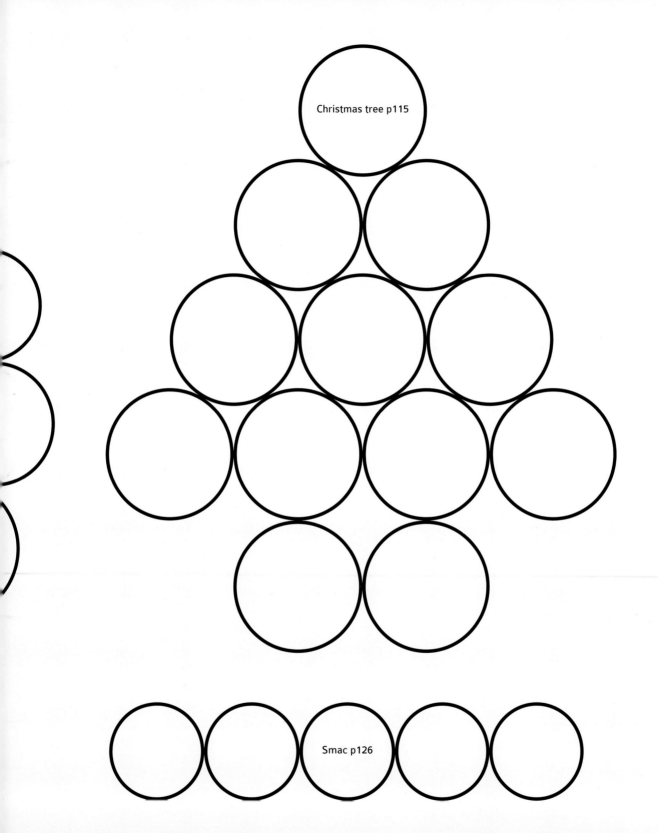

Christmas tree p115

Smac p126

index

suppliers

For information on equipment, templates
and technique videos
www.lorettaliu.com

Kenwood food mixers
www.kenwoodworld.com

Valrhona chocolate
www.valrhona.com
www.valrhona-chocolate.com

Cake lace
www.thecakedecoratingcompany.co.uk

Sugarflair food colouring pastes
www.sugarflair.com

Whole Foods Market (UK, USA and Canada)
www.wholefoods.com

Silpat silicone mats
www.silpat.com

UK cake and decorating supplies
www.cakecraftshop.co.uk
www.lakeland.co.uk

USA cake and decorating supplies
www.cake-stuff.com
www.wilton.com

acknowledgements

I am very thankful to have been given the chance to write a book. It's something I have wanted to do since I was young. I always dreamed of teaching, but being dyslexic makes writing difficult for me. Words puzzle me sometimes, so putting this book together was a huge challenge for me.

I am very grateful to Ryland Peters & Small. They have been extremely supportive and very encouraging, and have helped me put this book together. I am so grateful to Julia, Iona, Paul and Kate, my editor. The photography team was amazing to work with. Thanks to Maja for the stunning pictures and to Tony for the prop styling – you were both so passionate about my recipes.

I would also like to thank my friends and family. My husband has been really patient and my 8-year-old son, who always questioned what I was putting together and gave me endless ideas for patterns and flavours I could create. Thanks also to the rest of my family, including my mother and siblings, who have always supported me.

Thank you to my trusted pâtisserie stagiaire, Polly Chan, who is also my graphic designer – she has helped design all the templates for this book and many more on our website. Thanks also to the rest of my team – Ashim, Ichen and Tip Betelli.

I am very grateful to Debbie White for supplying Claire Bowman's Cake Lace from The Cake Decorating Company, to Marie Van Branteghem for supplying me with Valrhona chocolates and to Andrew Gravett of the Valrhona team for his amazing chocolate knowledge. Thank you Penny Jones of Kenwood for supporting our Cookery Club all these years and supplying us with the equipment used in this cookbook.

Finally, thank you to Jason Atherton for writing the foreword to this book.